9 AFRICAN AMERICAN INVENTORS

Achievers: African Americans In Science and Technology

9 AFRICAN AMERICAN INVENTORS

Robert C. Hayden

Twenty-First Century Books

A Division of Henry Holt and Company
New York

Twenty-First Century Books
A Division of Henry Holt and Company, Inc.
115 West 18th Street
New York, NY 10011

Henry Holt® and colophon are trademarks of
Henry Holt and Company, Inc.
Publishers since 1866

Published in Canada by Fitzhenry & Whiteside Ltd.,
195 Allstate Parkway, Markham, Ontario L3R 4T8.

Cover photo by Robert Houser/Comstock Inc.
Portrait illustrations by Richard Loehle

Library of Congress Cataloging-in-Publication Data

Hayden, Robert C.
9 African-American Inventors
Illustrated by Richard Loehle

Includes index.

Summary: Chronicles the achievements of nine Afro-Americans
responsible for inventions related to important parts of modern
life, such as refrigeration, electric lighting, and transportation.

1. Afro-American inventors—United States—Biography—Juvenile
literature. [1. Inventors. 2. Afro-Americans—Biography.]
I. Loehle, Richard, ill. II. Title. III. Title: Nine African-American
inventors. IV. Title: African-American inventors. V. Series: Hayden,
Robert C., Achievers: African Americans in Science and Technology.

T39.H39 1992 509.2'273—dc20 [B] 91-44193 CIP AC

ISBN 0-8050-2133-7

First Edition—1970

Printed in Mexico
All first editions are printed on acid-free paper ∞.

10 9 8 7 6

CONTENTS

FOREWORD

This book is about men and women who possessed the rare gift of invention. Invention, according to Webster's dictionary, is "the power to conceive and present new combinations of facts or ideas, to devise new methods or instruments." An invention is something that did not exist before the inventor came up with the idea. An invention is "an original." It's new. It's a "first." It must be useful and serve a definite purpose.

A U.S. patent for an invention is a grant of a property right. It is a protection given by the U.S. government to the inventor (or his or her heirs) to prevent unauthorized use of and profit from the invention by others. The right given by the patent grant is "the right to exclude others from making, using, or selling" the invention.

The patent protection is for 17 years from the date the patent is granted by the U.S. Patent Office, providing the inventor pays a maintenance fee to the office.*

More than 5 million patents have been issued by the U.S. Patent Office since it was established in 1791. Every year, the Patent Office awards more than 80,000 patent grants to inventors.

Before an inventor can even think about manufacturing, selling, and making money from an invention, he or she has to invest much time and money. Getting a U.S.

patent is a complicated first step. This usually involves building a model of the invention, having a professionally prepared drawing of the invention made, having a lawyer draw up a legal document describing the invention, and doing a search to be sure that no one else has patented the same invention.

(The search itself can cost from $100 to $250. Once all this is done, the inventor can file for a patent by paying a basic fee of $370.)

Frustration with some everyday problem in the home or work place usually sparks the need for a solution by the would-be inventor. Having decided to tackle the problem, inventors work at different solutions. Early inventors often worked alone or sometimes with a partner. Today, most inventors are engineers or scientists working with a team of people in a research laboratory. But the role of the individual as an inventor, with or without technical training, is still essential. Like those men and women you will read about in this book, individual inventors still play an important role in our society.

Every day, we use tools and objects in the home, in school, on the way to work, and at play—such everyday inventions as the traffic light and the wooden golf tee. They were invented by people like those featured in this book. Garrett Morgan invented the first three-way traffic signal, and Dr. George Grant invented the golf tee. Both were African Americans.

Throughout the history of the United States, far too little attention and recognition has been given to the many inventions of African-American people. Each of the men and women presented here is an example of the creativity, aspirations, and struggles that have shaped our country. Each of them has made a contribution to the industrial, technological, social, and economic progress of America. They were part of its making.

And when all Americans—young and old, black and white—come to know these men and women, we will have a greater understanding and respect for America and all of its citizens.

Robert C. Hayden
Boston, Massachusetts
1992

* Why is a patent granted for 17 years? Patent protection was one of the first pieces of legislation signed into law by George Washington in 1791. At the time, an apprenticeship (an apprentice is someone who is learning a trade or occupation) lasted seven years. Congress decided to provide protection for an inventor for the period of two apprenticeships. But some congressmen wanted the opportunity for an inventor to renew patents for another seven years. Finally, a compromise was passed, and patent protection was offered for a single term of 17 years.

INVENTIONS AND THE AFRICAN AMERICAN

Eli Whitney invented the cotton gin.
True or false?

Since 1792, most people have learned and believed this statement. American history books give Whitney full credit for inventing a machine that separates cotton fibers from seeds.

For a person to prove that an invention is his or hers alone, the inventor must be awarded a patent from the U.S. Patent Office. A patent is a grant from the U.S. government giving an inventor all rights to an invention.

However, even though Eli Whitney received a patent and full credit for the first cotton gin, he may not have been the true inventor. Instead, the real inventor may well have been an enslaved African who worked on a southern cotton plantation.

Eli Whitney was a native of New England who went south to study law and to be a teacher on a cotton plantation. He noticed how difficult it was to separate the seeds from cotton by hand. The work was hard and slow. Only a few pounds of cotton a day could be cleaned this way.

On one of his trips to Georgia, Whitney saw a crude comb-like instrument that loosened the seeds from cotton. It had been made and was being used by a slave whose name was Sam. As the story goes, Sam had learned how to make this labor-saving tool from his father. Eli Whitney improved upon and perfected the invention.

Until this time, the United States was shipping about 138,000 pounds of cotton to different parts of the world each year. Several years later, with the cotton gin in use, the United States exported about 6 million pounds a year.

Who was the real inventor of the cotton gin—a black man or a white man? This question can be asked about many inventions of the 1700s and 1800s. We will never know the whole truth about the cotton gin or, for that matter, about other inventions by black people. Their ideas were often stolen by their white masters.

Before the end of the Civil War (1865), noteworthy inventions by African Americans were not numerous. For most slaves, the foremost question was how to gain their freedom. They used their intelligence and vision to devise plans to escape from slavery and to interest others in gaining freedom. Many free blacks worked to save their enslaved "brothers and sisters." They did so by developing their literary and speaking abilities rather than by becoming machinists, engineers, or inventors.

During this period, most of the mechanical industries of the South used slave labor. Bits and pieces of history show that many of the tools of the day were designed by slaves. They invented various kinds of equipment to lessen the burden of their daily work. None of these, however, could be patented by the U.S. Patent Office. Worthwhile ideas by blacks were forever lost because of the attitude of the federal government at the time.

In 1858, Jeremiah S. Black, then attorney general of the United States, ruled that since a patent was a contract between the government and the inventor and since a slave was not a U.S. citizen, a slave could neither make a contract with the government nor assign an invention to his or her master.

For this reason, it has been impossible to discover the contributions of the many unnamed slaves whose creative skills added to the industrial and technological growth of this country.

Jo Anderson, one of the slaves on the plantation of Cyrus McCormick, is said to have made an important contribution to the McCormick grain harvester. Yet he is only credited in official records as being a handyman or helper to McCormick.

In 1862, a slave owned by Jefferson Davis, then president of the Confederacy, invented a propeller for ocean vessels. With a model of his invention, the slave showed remarkable mechanical skill in both woodworking and metalworking. He was unable to get a patent on his propeller, but the merits of his invention were reported in many southern newspapers. The propeller was finally used in ships of the Confederate navy.

The national ban on patents for slaves did not apply to inventions by "free persons of color." So, when James Forten (1776-1842) perfected a new device for handling sails, he had no trouble getting a patent from the government. From his invention, Forten was able to earn a good living for himself and his family. The same was true of another free black, Norbert Rillieux.

The first African American known to receive a U.S. patent was Thomas L. Jennings. Working as a tailor in New York City, he was granted a patent in 1821 for a method of dry-cleaning clothes called "dry scouring." Born free in New York City in 1791, he was an apprenticed tailor who moved on to establish his own tailoring and clothing business in New York's financial district.

In 1810, with other African-American businessmen, Jennings founded the New York African Society for Mutual Relief "to raise funds . . . towards the relief of widows and orphans of deceased members." As an early nineteenth-century civil rights leader, he held the position of assistant secretary for the First Annual Convention of People of Color in 1831 in Philadelphia. Jennings' success with his dry-cleaning technique was probably his only inventive effort. Like many other free blacks, he chose to devote his time and money to fighting for the freedom of those African Americans who were enslaved.

Henry Blair was the second black American to be granted a U.S. patent. He received his first patent in 1834 for a seed planter. In 1836, Blair received a second patent for a corn harvester. In both cases, he was described in the official records as "a colored man."

Following the Civil War, the growth of industry in this country was tremendous. Much of this growth was made possible by inventions made by both blacks and whites. It is estimated that by the year 1913 a thousand inventions had been patented by African Americans in such diverse fields as industrial machinery, rapid transportation, and electrical equipment.

The number of inventions made by black people increased after the Civil War, when legal slavery ended and fewer obstacles stood in the way. Industrial opportunities were widely available, and the records prove that blacks had just as much inventive ability as whites.

It is interesting to see how the inventions of black people have been recorded. Since Blair received his second patent, the U.S. Patent Office has never kept a record of whether an inventor was black or white. However, on two different occasions, the Patent Office has sought this information. The first inquiry was made by the Patent Office in 1900 for a U.S. commission that was preparing an exhibit on black Americans for a fair in Paris. The second was made in 1913 at the request of a commission planning a freedom exhibit in Philadelphia.

In both instances, the Patent Office sent out several thousand letters to patent lawyers, manufacturing firms, and the various newspapers edited by blacks. The people who received the letters were asked to inform the Patent Office of any patents granted for inventions by blacks.

The first letter sent out by the U.S. Patent Office read as follows:

DEPARTMENT OF THE INTERIOR

United States Patent Office

Washington D.C., January 26, 1900

Dear Sir:

This Office is endeavoring to obtain information concerning patents issued to colored inventors, in accordance with a request from the United States Commission to the Paris Exposition of 1900, to be used in preparing the "Negro Exhibit."

To aid in this work, you are requested to send to this Office, in the enclosed envelope, which will not require a postage stamp, the names of any colored inventors you can furnish, together with the date of grant, title of invention, and patent number, so that a list without errors can be prepared.

You will confer a special favor by aiding in the preparation of this list by filling in the blank form below, and sending in any replies as promptly as possible. Should you be unable to furnish any data, will you kindly inform us of that fact?

Very respectfully,

O. H. Duell
Commissioner of Patents

The replies were numerous. The information showed that a very large number of African Americans had contacted lawyers about their inventions. Even so, many were unable to get patents because they lacked the necessary funds to apply for them. Some had actually obtained patents, but the records of most lawyers were poorly kept. So the names and inventions of many blacks were lost.

Patents were often taken out in the name of the lawyer. A large number of African-American inventors would allow this to happen because they felt that if the racial identity of the inventor were known, it would lower the value of a patented invention. Yet more than a thousand patents were fully identified by the name of the inventor, date, patent number, and title of invention as being owned by blacks.

These patents represent inventions in nearly every branch of industrial arts, such as household goods, mechanical appliances, electrical devices, and chemical compounds. In the beginning, agricultural and home utensils were most common. But gradually these inventors widened the field of their efforts.

The most significant black inventors following the Civil War were Elijah McCoy, Jan E. Matzeliger, Granville T. Woods, Lewis H. Latimer, and Garrett A. Morgan.

- Elijah McCoy, who held more than 50 patents, was born to slave parents who had escaped to Canada. McCoy's greatest contribution was the lubricating cup, a device that fed oil to machinery while it was still running.

- Jan E. Matzeliger developed a new machine that completely changed the manufacturing of shoes in this country. (Unable to sell his invention himself, Matzeliger sold the rights to his machine to the United Shoe Machinery Company.)

- Lewis H. Latimer worked with Alexander Graham Bell and Thomas Edison. He wrote a book that explained how Edison's electric light worked and also served as Edison's expert witness in many patent cases.

- Garrett A. Morgan invented a gas mask used in World War I. Later, Morgan created an automatic traffic light that brought greater safety to people traveling on streets and highways.

In addition to the lives and works of these men, the stories of several other inventors are presented in this book. Two of them, Lewis Temple and Norbert Rillieux, lived before the Civil War. Temple invented a harpoon that brought sweeping changes to the whaling industry, and Rillieux's invention revolutionized the processing of sugar.

Frederick Jones invented a new refrigeration unit that made possible the truck transportation of perishable foods until they reached the supermarket shelves. Granville T. Woods, who is sometimes called the "Black Edison," held more than 35 patents on electrical devices sold to such companies as American Bell Telephone, General Electric, and Westinghouse Air Brake.

And not all African-American inventors are men. The work of Valerie Thomas and many others reminds us of the important, if often overlooked, contributions that African-American women have made to our society.

Readers interested in more information on the patents listed in the appendices may find detailed descriptions in U.S. patent records. (These are kept at many public and college libraries.)

The present generation should find inspiration and encouragement in the stories of the inventors presented here. The future historian will find a faithful portrayal of the contributions made by African-American inventors and the times in which they lived and worked.

GARRETT A. MORGAN

1

On July 25, 1916, a violent explosion ripped through Tunnel No. 5 of the Cleveland Waterworks. The tunnel was 250 feet below the surface of Lake Erie. At the moment of the explosion, more than 30 men were working there. Deadly gases, heavy smoke, dust, and debris quickly filled the underground space. The men were trapped inside the tunnel.

Firemen, doctors, nurses, policemen, and waterworks employees gathered at the tunnel's entrance. Relatives and friends of the trapped men stood by grimly. No one knew the fate of the trapped workers—it wasn't likely that anyone could stay alive for more than a few hours. Someone would have to enter the tunnel if the men were to be saved, but the heavy smoke and poisonous gases made it impossible for anyone to try. There seemed to be little chance of rescuing the workers.

At that moment, Garrett A. Morgan was resting at his Cleveland home. Someone at the scene of the tunnel explosion remembered that recently a black man had been demonstrating a gas inhalator, trying to interest manufacturers in his invention. In fact, Morgan had received a patent for this invention four years earlier and had been awarded First Grand Prize for his inhalator at an international safety and sanitation exposition in New York City. However, he had not been successful in selling his device.

Now, someone contacted Morgan and asked him to come to the tunnel immediately with several of his gas inhalators. He arrived at the Lake Erie tunnel with his brother. Quickly, they and two other volunteers donned gas masks and descended into the tunnel in search of the trapped men. They were the only ones able to enter the smoke-and-gas-filled tunnel and reach the bodies of the unconscious and dead workers.

The gas inhalators allowed them to breathe clean air that was carried in a pouch of the inhalator. Morgan led the rescue team in and out of the tunnel many times. Together, they saved the lives of 32 people by carrying them out of the tunnel to the waiting crowd.

This act of heroism thrust Garrett Morgan before the public. Manufacturers and fire departments across the country suddenly became interested in his gas inhalator, or gas mask as we would call it today. Orders for the mask poured into Cleveland from fire companies all over the United States.

Morgan was asked to talk about and demonstrate his invention in many cities and towns. For his courage, he was awarded a solid gold, diamond-studded medal by the city of Cleveland. But, more important, his heroism also helped to prove the value of his invention.

However, when it became known that Garrett Morgan was a black man, many orders for his gas mask were canceled. When he traveled in the South, it was necessary for Morgan to have a white man demonstrate his invention while he passed himself off as an American Indian.

A Breath of Fresh Air

Garrett Morgan was not discouraged by the racial discrimination he faced as an African-American inventor, and he went on to perfect his first gas mask. During World War I, American soldiers used Morgan's improved mask in battle to protect themselves from deadly chlorine fumes. Morgan's invention saved many lives.

Morgan received his first patent for a safety hood and smoke protector in 1912. During the next two years, his "Style One Helmet," as it was called, passed many tests successfully. It met the approval of many fire chiefs in the United States and Canada.

Morgan's safety helmet was designed to protect firefighters from heavy smoke and dangerous chemicals. It could be put on in seven seconds and taken off in three. Clean air was supplied from a bag of air suspended in the rear by two tubes leading from the hood. There was enough air in the bag to permit a person to stay in the midst of suffocating gases and smoke for 15 to 20 minutes.

An article that appeared in the *New Orleans Times-Picyayune* on October 22, 1914, read as follows:

ABOUT MORGAN'S
NATIONAL SAFETY HOOD
AND SMOKE PROTECTOR
Spectacular Exhibit

One of the spectacular shows of the day was given by the National Safety Device Company with a Morgan Helmet. A canvas tent, close flapped and secure, was erected on an open space and inside the tent a fire started. The fuel was made up of tar, sulfur, formaldehyde, and manure, and the character of the smoke was the thickest and most evil smelling imaginable. Charles P. Salan, former director of public works of Cleveland under Mayor Johnson, conducted the tests.

Fitting a big canvas affair that had the appearance of a diver's helmet on the head of "Big Chief" Mason, a full-blooded Indian, Mr. Salan sent the Indian under the flaps into the smoke-filled tent. The smoke was thick enough to strangle an elephant, but Mason lingered around in the suffocating atmosphere for a full twenty minutes and experienced no inconvenience. He came out after the test "as good as new," and a little later gave another exhibition. The Morgan Helmet is fitted with a long hose that reaches to the ground, where there is always the current of fresh air, no matter the thickness of the smoke.

In competitive tests, the Morgan Safety Smoke Hood easily proved itself superior. Here is what Fire Chief J. J. Mulcahey, of Yonkers, New York, reported:

In a competitive test made at our headquarters, Saturday, September 15, 1914, between another make and the Morgan National Safety Helmet, the "other make" demonstrator remained in a gas-and-smoke-filled room for

14 minutes, and the Morgan demonstrator remained in the same room for 25 minutes—and when he came out, he did not seem to be at all uncomfortable. We tried them both, and we all prefer the Morgan Helmet; and I immediately placed an order for six Morgan Helmets upon the merits of the helmet and its demonstration, at a price of $25 each, for general use in our department.

Fire Chief J. T. Mertz, of Akron, Ohio, had this to say:

What is the use of fighting fires all night when you can stop them in minutes? Two men with a Morgan Smoke Hood and a good fire extinguisher can do more in the first 15 minutes than a whole company can in the next half hour.

A Successful Tinker

Garrett Morgan was born on March 4, 1877, in Paris, Kentucky. His mother had been a slave who was freed by the Emancipation Proclamation in 1863. He grew up on a farm with his brothers and sisters and attended school through grade six.

When Morgan was 14 years old, he left home and traveled to Cincinnati, Ohio, to look for a job. There, he worked for four years as a general handyman for a wealthy landowner. During this time, Morgan hired a tutor to help him with his English grammar. In 1895, he moved again, this time to Cleveland, Ohio, which was to be his home for the rest of his life.

Morgan's first job in Cleveland was that of a sewing machine adjuster for a clothing manufacturer. He loved to tinker with machinery, and his skill at fixing mechanical things provided him with jobs at several different firms.

In 1907, Morgan decided to start a business for himself, and he opened a shop for repairing and selling sewing machines. He was a smart businessman, and two years later he opened his own tailoring shop. He hired 32 workers and began making coats, suits, and dresses with the various sewing devices he had built.

One day, just before supper time, Garrett Morgan was experimenting at home with a liquid that would give a high polish to sewing machine needles. A good polish would prevent a needle from scorching material as it stitched. When Mrs. Morgan called her husband to the dinner table, he hastily wiped the polishing liquid that was on his hands on a piece of wiry pony-fur cloth lying on his workbench. When he returned from the dinner table, Morgan noticed that the wiry fibers of the cloth where he had wiped his hands were quite straight.

Being naturally curious, Morgan began to think about what had happened to the fibers of the cloth. His next-door neighbor had an Airedale dog, and Morgan asked his neighbor to let him try some of his needle polish on the dog's fur. The same thing happened—the dog's hair became so straight that Morgan's neighbor hardly recognized his own pet.

Next, Morgan tried the fluid on his own hair, applying a little bit at first, then gradually applying it to all of his hair. The result was the same. Garrett Morgan had discovered, by chance, a process for straightening hair. He changed his "magic" liquid into a cream and organized the G. A. Morgan Hair Refining Company to introduce his hair-straightening process to the public. He also marketed a black hair oil stain for men whose hair was turning gray and a curved-tooth iron comb that he invented in 1910 for straightening women's hair.

Morgan's business enterprise prospered. He was able to buy his own home and an automobile. It is believed that he was the first black person in Cleveland to own a car. Undoubtedly, his experience in driving through the streets of Cleveland led him to another invention, one which is still with us today on street corners and highways across our country—the three-way traffic light.

A Signal for the Future

Morgan was a man who was always experimenting with new ideas. On November 20, 1923, his tinkering paid off when he was awarded a patent for inventing a three-way traffic signal.

The "Go-Stop" signals in general use before Morgan's invention were not practical because there was no neutral position. In other words, the signal indicated either stop or go. There was no in-between signal as we have it today (the yellow light). And without a traffic officer present, the signals could be ignored completely.

Morgan's traffic signal was designed so that the stop and go signs could be left in a position that enabled traffic to move in all directions even without an officer. This idea also solved another problem. The traffic officer often failed to change the signal promptly. The resulting confusion delayed both drivers and pedestrians.

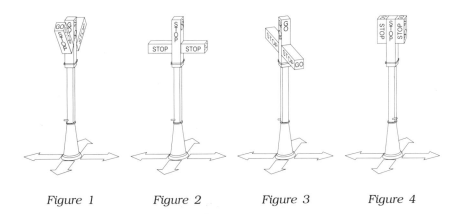

Figure 1   Figure 2   Figure 3   Figure 4

GARRETT MORGAN'S
THREE-WAY TRAFFIC SIGNAL
Patented 1923

When Morgan's signal was at the half-mast position, as is shown in Figure 1, cars using caution could move in all directions—north, south, east, and west—even when a traffic officer was not present. The half-mast position was also used at night to mark dangerous intersections. When a driver approached Morgan's signal in the half-mast position, he or she would do just what today's driver would do when approaching a blinking yellow light—slow down and proceed with caution.

Figure 2 shows traffic moving east and west while the north and south traffic would be at a standstill. To stop traffic moving east and west, the signal post was rotated so that "Go" faced north and south, as shown in Figure 3. Figure 4 shows the position of the signal that stopped traffic in all directions to allow pedestrians to cross the street in safety.

Today's system of traffic light signals makes possible the orderly movement of vehicles on our highways and streets. It also provides for the safety of pedestrians crossing at busy intersections.

In a simpler way, Morgan's signal did the same thing. He sold the rights to his invention to the General Electric Corporation for $40,000, and it became the forerunner of the overhead and sidewalk red, green, and yellow lights that we use every day.

Safety First

It would be difficult to estimate how many lives have been saved because of Garrett Morgan's inventions. Many veterans of World War I certainly owed their lives to the gas masks they wore on the battlefield. The electric light signal system used in this country has been responsible for protecting lives on our streets, highways, and railways.

Morgan received several medals and citations for his inventions. The National Safety Device Company awarded him a First Grand Prize for his gas inhalator. The U.S. government gave him a citation for his traffic signal device. The International Association of Fire Chiefs awarded him a gold medal and made him an honorary member.

In 1943, Garrett Morgan contracted glaucoma, an eye disease that gradually made him almost blind during the later years of his life. Each year until 1959, he traveled alone by train to the Mayo Clinic in Rochester, New York, for treatment of his eye condition. Garrett Morgan, a man who saved so many lives, died in 1963.

Five months after Morgan's death, his granddaughter, Karen Morgan, wrote a biographical sketch of her famous grandfather. She recalled his life in this way:

> Coming from a poor family, G. A. Morgan did all he could to enrich both his life and that of his family. He was a jolly man, although he had his stern moments and was very quick tempered and outspoken. . . . He gained some foes, but he had many friends. . . .
>
> Mr. Morgan was a down-to-earth, practical man. He worked hard for everything he ever did or accomplished. . . . After he lost 90 percent of his sight, he made constant use of his mind and his hands. He always kept himself busy. . . . With all of his achievements, recognition, and possessions, one fact remained to be true until his last breath: . . . he was a plain man, . . . proud to be an American, proud of his race.
>
> His last goal or ambition in life was to be able to attend the Emancipation Centennial which was to be held in Chicago, in August of 1963. His wish was not fulfilled, however, as he died one month before it was to take place.

LEWIS TEMPLE

2

During the days of American whaling, whalers kept a diary of each voyage. Probably the most valuable and interesting records of the old whaling days are found in the logbooks kept by captains. Their voyages were long, tedious, and dangerous. Some lasted as long as four years. The following accounts were taken from a page in an old whaler's logbook. There were many reports like these:

August 2, 1761. Latitude 45° 54' N., longitude 53° 37' W., saw sperm-whale; killed one.

August 6. Spoke to John Clasberry; he had got one hundred and five barrels; told us Seth Folger had got one hundred and fifty barrels. Spoke with two Nantucket men; they had got one whale between them; they told us that Jenkens and Dunham had got four whales, and Allen and Pease had got two whales between them. Latitude 42° 57' N.

August 28. Saw spermaceti, but could not strike. Latitude 43°.

August 30. Saw spermaceti; foggy; lost sight of him.

August 31. Saw spermaceti plenty; squally, and thunder.

September 2. Saw spermaceti; foggy and dark.

September 3. This morning at eight saw a spermaceti; got into her two short warps and the tow iron, but she ran away. In the afternoon came across her again; got another iron in, but she went away.

September 5. Saw spermaceti; chased, but could not strike.

September 6. Saw whales; struck one, but never saw her again.

September 7. Saw small school of spermaceti. Captain Shearman struck one out of the vessel, and killed her. Latitude 43°.

Wooden block stamps were used to record the number of whales sighted and captured. When a whale was captured, the logbook page was stamped with the figure of a full whale. A half-whale figure meant that the whale had gotten away.

If you were to look through the pages of a logbook from a whaling voyage, you would probably count more half whales than whole whales—and you would begin to realize that although many whales were seen, few were actually caught—for the methods of capture were far from being perfect.

To capture and kill a whale, two basic weapons were used—a harpoon and a lance. The job of the harpoon was not to kill, but to hook the whale, as a fishhook does a fish. The long, spear-like lance was the killing weapon. Only on rare occasions did the harpoon itself actually kill the whale.

When a whaleboat was close to a whale, the harpooner would dart his harpoon into its blubber. Attached to the harpoon was some 1,300 feet of rope. Once the whale was "struck," the rope was tied to the boat. The harpooned whale would dive down into the water and dash off at a great speed, towing the boat with its crew aboard.

Sometimes, the tow-line would be attached to a heavy wooden drag (or weight) that the whale pulled through the water as it tried to escape. Eventually, the whale would tire from pulling the load, and once again the whaleboat could approach the animal. The lance would be thrown like a spear. The harpooner hoped to hit the lungs of the whale to kill it.

But many times the lancer would not get a chance to throw his weapon. Often, the pointed, barbed head of the harpoon was no match for the tremendous strength of the whale as it dove and twisted through the water, dragging the boat. The strength of a whale was so great that harpoons were often twisted into fantastic shapes or broken. Frequently, the whale pulled free from the hooked head of the harpoon and escaped. Sometimes, the harpoon simply slipped out of the hole that it had made in the whale's fleshy blubber. Many whales were lost this way.

A New Era in Whaling

In 1848, Lewis Temple, a black man from New Bedford, Massachusetts, invented a new type of harpoon. It had a movable head and worked in such a way as to prevent a harpooned whale from slipping loose from the hook and escaping. The head of Temple's harpoon became "locked" in the whale's flesh, and the only way to free it was to cut it loose after the whale was killed.

Catching whales was an ancient European industry, dating as far back as the twelfth and thirteenth centuries. Whaling was brought to the New England colonies by some of the earliest settlers. The exact date that whaling began in the New Bedford, Massachusetts, area is uncertain, but it was at least as early as 1746.

During the 1800s, New Bedford was the capital of the whaling industry in America. The products that came from whales—oil, meat, and whalebone—were important to the country's economy. In 1846, more than 700 whaling ships sailed from the 23 ports located from Maine to New Jersey. Many of these ports gave up whaling after 1847, but the fleets from New Bedford continued to grow.

Whaling reached its peak in this area in 1857, with 329 whaleships employing more than 10,000 men from New Bedford and nearby towns. Lewis Temple's toggle had become the standard harpoon of the whaling industry.

It was not until Temple invented what became known as the Toggle Iron (and, later, Temple's Iron) that real change was made in the method of catching whales. In 1820, an authority on whaling wrote that "many ingenious persons had tried to improve the whaling harpoon; and although various changes had been devised, they had all given place to the simplicity of the ancient harpoon."

Soon after Temple invented his first toggle harpoon, it became the accepted whaling weapon. It was made into more complex harpoons, such as those shot by a gun, but was never improved upon in any basic way.

In 1926, Clifford Ashley, an authority on the history of whaling, wrote: "It is safe to say that the 'Temple Toggle' was the most important single invention in the whole history of whaling. It resulted in the capture of a far greater proportion of the whales that were struck than had before been possible."

Who was this African-American inventor whose device changed the nature of whaling practices, which in turn helped this country to prosper? He was not a whaler. He never went to sea. Some believe that he never even learned to write his name.

The Blacksmith and the Whale

Outfitting whaleships for a year or two of whale hunting was a huge and serious undertaking. It required the skills and work of many trades people, and during the 1800s many individuals in New Bedford were involved in it. There were sail makers, rope makers, oil barrel makers, and oar makers. There were the boat builders. And there were the blacksmiths, who hammered out whaling tools and weapons from hot iron and steel. Lewis Temple was one of these blacksmiths.

He was born in Richmond, Virginia, in the year 1800. Whether he was a free man or a slave in the South during his childhood and youth is not known. How he happened to land in New Bedford around 1830 is not certain either, but during the 1800s this city was one of the northern locations to which runaway slaves escaped. It was also one of the "stations" along the route of the Underground Railroad to Canada. The Underground Railroad was a network of homes and farms where antislavery people would hide escaping slaves.

Perhaps Temple was one of the more than 100,000 slaves who made their way to freedom along the route of the Underground Railroad between 1810 and 1850. Or perhaps he was already free and just decided to settle in New Bedford. In either case, in the late 1820s Temple was one of 315,000 free black people in the United States, and he was on his way to becoming successful.

By 1836, Lewis Temple was a well-known citizen in the village of New Bedford. He was married, had three children, and was working as a blacksmith. How Temple learned the metalwork trade is impossible to say, but we do know that many of the Africans who were brought to America as slaves were skilled crafts people.

By 1845, it seems that Temple was doing extremely well in the blacksmith business. He was able to build his own shop. The whaling business was booming at the time. The manufacture of whaling products was the third leading industry in Massachusetts, after shoes and textiles.

Undoubtedly, Temple knew and talked with whalers who came to his blacksmith shop to have harpoons and other whaling tools made. From these conversations, he learned about adventures at sea and the struggle of catching whales. Temple would probably also have learned that many whales escaped because the harpoon would not hold fast in the flesh of the whale.

Complaints about the old-style harpoon were increasing. The urgent need for a new and better harpoon was apparent to many people. Temple clearly recognized the problem and worked quietly away in his shop on a new type of harpoon, one that would not pull out of the whale's blubber when the whale pulled and tugged on the tow-line.

His solution was the toggle harpoon. What was a toggle harpoon and how did it work? How was it different from the harpoons that had been used before?

To Catch a Whale

A whaling harpoon can be thought of as having two parts—a head and a shank. The harpoon's length, from the tip of its pointed head to the end of the shank, was about 33 inches. The steel head was welded to a tough iron shank. The end of the shank was attached to the end of a wooden pole about six feet in length. The whale line (rope) was tied to the end of the shank where it joined the wooden handle.

The head was shaped with a hook or barb that was supposed to hold the whale. The barb, or flue as it was sometimes called, curved backward from the point of the harpoon head. (To get a good idea of what a flue is, look at the end of a fishhook.) Both single-flue and double-flue harpoons were used by American whalers. These two types of harpoons were handed down from English and Dutch whalers. They were the best harpoons American whalers had to work with for many years.

It is important to note that the flued head was fixed and immovable. This is where Lewis Temple made his big change. He made the barbed head movable. The head of his harpoon was mounted on the shank so that it turned after piercing the flesh of the whale. It turned, or toggled, at a right angle to the shank. This prevented the harpoon from being drawn out when the struck whale pulled away.

Above are harpoon heads used in whaling from its ancient beginning through Lewis Temple's era. From left to right: double flue, single flue, Temple Iron, improved Temple Iron.

Let's look at this toggle principle by another example. Suppose you had a coat with wooden peg buttons. If you simply pushed the peg-shaped buttons through the button holes, they wouldn't hold your coat very well. But if you turned each peg after pushing it through the eye-like slit, so that it turned at a right angle crossing the slit, then it would not slip back through the hole. Temple used this same principle in the design of his harpoon.

When Temple's Toggle Iron entered the whale, the barb was parallel with the shank. To hold the barbed head parallel until it had cut through the blubber, a wooden pin the size of a toothpick was used. It was placed in a hole that ran through the shank and the barb of the harpoon. Under the pull of the whale in its desperate attempt to escape, the wooden pin holding the barbed head in a fixed position was broken. This allowed the head to toggle, or turn, across the end of the shank and become firmly anchored. The head in this position was not likely to slip out of the blubber and was more secure than the fixed-head harpoon.

A History of the Toggle

It was difficult for a time to get many whalers to use Lewis Temple's novel design. Some whalers, reluctant to try something new and different, ridiculed Temple's invention and laughed it off. But after a little experience, most whaling captains were convinced that Temple's Toggle Iron was far superior to the ordinary barbed type, and it was adopted by the majority of American whalers.

Temple's harpoon was a simple device. In fact, the toggle idea in harpoons did not originate with him. And it is a wonder that it had not been used by American whalers before 1848. The toggle idea has had a strange history of appearance, disappearance, and reappearance in whaling. Archaeologists have discovered, in fact, that prehistoric man in northern Eurasia used a type of toggle harpoon.

Yet in the Middle Ages whalers lost or forgot the toggle method. It seems that Europeans during this period used harpoons that were even more primitive than those used by the Stone Age whalers of Norway. Only in the very remote regions of the Arctic and along the northerly coasts of the Pacific Ocean was the toggle harpoon continuously used. It was used by the Eskimos to catch the sea animals that supplied them with their meat.

The toggle head of the Eskimos' harpoons, which was made from bone, was a detachable device. It pulled off the shank and worked into the blubber as the whale pulled on the tow-line. During the seventeenth and eighteenth centuries, European whalers had a chance to observe the whaling tools of these Eskimos.

About 10 years before Lewis Temple's invention, some American whalers also had an opportunity to learn about the toggle harpoon. In 1835, new whaling grounds near Alaska were discovered. This opened up more water for thousands of whaleships. On trips to Alaska, American whalers met Eskimos and Pacific Coast Indians who were using a removable head toggle iron. Why the whalers never adopted the Eskimos' toggle is hard to explain.

Some experimental harpoons were tried and patented shortly before Lewis Temple's invention. These harpoons were exactly like the single-flue harpoons except that the diameter of the shank just in back of the head was much smaller than the rest of it. Instead of breaking off, the harpoon would bend inside the blubber. This bending, caused by the twisting of the whale as it tried to escape, produced a crude type of toggle.

If Lewis Temple had not invented the toggle harpoon, the single-flue harpoon probably would have remained the favorite weapon of American whale fishery. And whalers would have had to take their chances at killing the whale if they were lucky enough not to lose it.

Temple's Legacy

Temple's invention encouraged others to develop new harpoons. In the second half of the 1800s, more than 100 different patents on harpoons were issued by the U.S. Patent Office. Most of them involved only minor changes to Temple's original model. Even the harpoons that were shot from a gun had the basic toggle head.

One change to the original Temple Iron was made by a man named Macy, another blacksmith in New Bedford. He manufactured a harpoon so that the head swung outside or over the shank. Temple's toggle head swung inside the harpoon shank, the shank being forked over it. Macy's change made the toggle harpoon easier to manufacture.

For some unknown reason, Temple never patented his invention, and other blacksmiths were quick to copy the

Temple Toggle. There were some eight or more blacksmith shops in New Bedford during this time. One whalecraft maker in New Bedford made 30,000 toggle harpoons between 1848 and 1868.

After 1848, the pages of whaling logbooks began to take on a new look. The half-whale figures that were used to indicate that a whale had escaped did not appear as often. More full-whale figures appeared in the daily reports of whaling captains. In trip after trip, the Temple Iron was proving what it could do. In 1853, the whaleship *Ohio* returned home from the Arctic with 2,300 barrels of oil. In killing 21 bowhead whales, only 8 harpoons were used. All of them were Temple Irons.

Around 1852, Lewis Temple was making a fairly good living from the sale of his harpoons. But it was nowhere near the fortune that Temple could have made if he had patented his invention. He was, however, able to buy the building next to his home and set up a new blacksmith shop. Temple's business continued to grow, and he was becoming even more successful.

In 1854, a construction firm was hired to build Lewis Temple a new and bigger shop out of brick. This shop was never finished. One night, during the fall of 1853, Temple was walking near the site where his new shop was to be built. He stumbled over a board that was hidden by the darkness. The injuries Temple received were serious and prevented him from working. Money became a problem. In May 1854, at the age of 54, Lewis Temple died of the injuries from his fall.

Although the city of New Bedford voted to pay Temple $2,000 for the injury and the time lost from his work, the money was never paid. Temple died a poor man. When his estate was settled, there was practically no money left for his wife and children. His home, the blacksmith shop and its equipment, and the half-finished brick shop were used to pay his debts.

The only thing left was Lewis Temple's name and the harpoon that he had invented. But in the years following his death, it was proven beyond doubt that his harpoon had revolutionized the whaling industry.

Postscript

While growing up in New Bedford, Massachusetts, between 1937 and 1955, I never heard the name of Lewis Temple or learned about his contribution to whaling. Each day during my high-school years, I would pass by a statue on the lawn to the right-hand side of the New Bedford Public Library. It depicted a white man in a whaling boat holding a whaling harpoon. Yes, the Temple Toggle.

The statue was placed there in 1913, "In Honor of the Whalemen, Whose Skill, Hardihood and Daring Brought Fame and Fortune to New Bedford and Made Its Name Known in Every Seaport on the Globe." Most of the whalers in New Bedford were African-American and Cape Verdean men (from the Cape Verde Islands off the west coast of Africa). From that statue, one could never guess the role of black people in whaling history.

But in 1987 a life-sized statue of Lewis Temple holding his toggle harpoon was placed on the lawn to the left side of the library entrance. It was sculptured by the late James Toatley, an African-American artist.

So progress is being made.

R.C.H.

FREDERICK MCKINLEY JONES

3

On a hot summer night in 1937, Frederick McKinley Jones was trying to cool off by driving around a lake in the city of Minneapolis, Minnesota. He stopped his car to catch a breath of fresh air. The cool breeze coming off the lake provided much needed relief from the sweltering heat in the city.

But with his car windows down, mosquitoes swarmed in on him, and Jones was forced to close them. Then, the heat inside the car became unbearable. So Fred Jones left the lakeside and headed home. As he drove along the highway, he asked himself why someone had not invented a device to air-condition a car.

The next morning, Fred Jones arrived early at the public library in Minneapolis. He located all the books he could find on refrigeration and air conditioning. Finding no evidence that anyone had ever developed an air conditioner for an automobile, Jones began to sketch a design for one. A week later, he showed his plans for a car air conditioner to his boss, Joseph A. Numero.

Numero was not impressed. "It would be too heavy," he told Jones. "Also, it would be too expensive to make, and I don't think anyone would buy it. Besides, we're in the business of making equipment for theaters, so let's stick to that."

Fred Jones put his plans for a car air cooler aside. But the idea stayed in his mind. He kept thinking about it and continued to read all he could find on the science of refrigeration and air cooling.

About a year later, Numero was playing golf on a hot midsummer day with two friends. One friend was in the trucking business; the other was in the air conditioning business. Mr. Werner, the owner of the Werner Transportation Company, had recently lost a truckload of chickens when the big ice blocks for keeping the meat cold melted before the truck had reached the market.

This was not the first time that Werner had lost a shipment of food this way, and he shared his frustration with his golfing companions. It seemed quite surprising to him that someone had invented an air conditioner to cool buildings but not the inside of a truck.

"Why can't someone make a machine that will keep the inside of a truck cool?" Werner wanted to know. "It seems to me that if a movie theater can be cooled off, then surely someone ought to be able to cool a truckload of chickens without having to use ice."

The air conditioning expert explained to Werner that, so far, attempts to do this had failed. The jarring and jolting of a truck on the highway made it impossible for a mechanical refrigerator to work properly.

As Numero drove his ball off the tee, he turned to Werner and told him jokingly, "I'll build you a refrigerator for your truck." This was quite a big boast for Numero, who was in the business of manufacturing motion picture equipment. The threesome walked off the tee onto the fairway. The conversation turned back to golf. Little did Numero realize that the trucker had taken his remark seriously, and neither had he remembered Jones' idea for an air cooler for automobiles.

A few weeks later, Werner called Numero to tell him that he had purchased a new truck and was ready for Numero to work on a cooling unit for it. The same day, a shiny, new van appeared in the parking lot of Numero's firm—Cinema Supplies, Inc.

Needless to say, Numero was dumbfounded. He called his friend Werner back on the phone. "I was just fooling around—really, just kidding—when I said I could build a refrigerator for your truck," Numero explained.

Frederick Jones, an engineer at Numero's firm, had noticed the truck when it pulled into the company parking lot and overheard the telephone conversation that his boss was having with Werner. It was clear to Jones that his boss, who knew only about making sound equipment for movie theaters, was stuck with a truck in which he was supposed to install an air conditioning unit.

Seeing that Numero was embarrassed, Jones climbed into the truck and took some measurements. He worked throughout most of the night making calculations. The next day, Jones told his boss that he could build the kind of cooling unit that Werner wanted.

Fred Jones knew that the earlier truck refrigeration units had been jolted into pieces. They had been "such big clunks," as he described them, and they took up too much space inside the truck itself. Jones had some experience in building shock-proof and vibration-proof gadgets. After much figuring, he came up with a light, compact, and sturdy unit that he thought would do the job.

He installed this unit under the truck, but it quickly broke down as it became mud-clogged. So he mounted a similar unit to the forehead of the truck above the cab, where it would be out of the way and could use space that had been wasted. It worked.

This invention led to the formation of a new firm by Numero and Jones. Their company began to manufacture a compact, automatic, shock-proof air conditioner for the truck transportation of foods. Today, this firm is a thriving company called Thermo King, located in Minneapolis.

Jones' device was the first practical truck refrigeration unit, and it helped to transform the food and transportation industries. It created new markets for many crops and influenced the eating habits of countless people. Frozen foods were now available to more individuals. And during World War II, a portable refrigeration unit designed by Fred Jones was used on the battlefields of Europe to preserve medicine that saved the lives of injured soldiers.

Learning the Hard Way

Frederick Jones became a top ranking engineer and inventor the hard way. He was an orphan for most of his boyhood. His mother had died when he was only an infant; his father died when Fred was nine years old. After his father's death, Fred left his birthplace, Cincinnati, Ohio, and went to live with a priest, Father Ryan, in Kentucky. There, he lived in a rectory where he did odd jobs for the priest and attended school through grade six. When Jones was 16, he decided to look for a job.

When he left the rectory, the first big automobiles were beginning to appear. Jones was fascinated by these machines and hitched a ride in one at every chance. He developed a burning desire to work with them—to use his mind and his hands, to touch the mechanical parts under the hood. Jones figured that the only way to do this was to get a job as an auto mechanic.

So, without experience or much education, he began his search. Jones returned to Cincinnati, where he was able to convince a garage owner that he was a skilled mechanic. The owner agreed to try him out on the following Monday morning. But Jones couldn't wait until then to get his hands on the cars. He showed up at 6 A.M. the next day—a Saturday—and waited for his new employer to open up the shop.

Jones had to prove himself. Although he didn't have much schooling, he had a keen, inventive mind and an ability for understanding machinery. When he came to a problem in his work that stumped him, he went to the library and studied books on the subject. This became a habit of his, and he practiced it throughout his life. Hard work and serious study paid off for the young mechanic.

Three years later, Fred Jones became the foreman of the automobile shop. Now, he wanted to work on racing cars. Auto racing was becoming a popular sport at the time, and the successful racer needed a car that would not fall apart at high speeds. Fred and his crew could take a bare chassis (car frame), pull the steering wheel down to a sporty angle, change the gears, install a foot throttle and bucket seats, juggle other parts around—and wind up with a racer. Fred had built a couple of speedy racers by the time he was 19, but his boss thought that he was too young to race. So others drove his cars instead.

One day, Fred could not resist the temptation to be at the track to watch one of the cars that he had built. He ducked out of the garage without his boss's permission and headed for the track. It was worth it to him since the racer that he had worked on so hard and had kept in top condition won the race.

But Fred's boss did not like the idea of one of his mechanics sneaking off. He decided to lay Fred off for a while to teach him a lesson. This was hard for the young racing enthusiast to take. So Fred quit his job and headed for Chicago to see the sights of a big city.

From the Farm to the Racetrack

On his way back to Cincinnati from Chicago, Fred Jones somehow boarded the wrong train. At daybreak, he found himself in the town of Effingham, Illinois. Jones decided to explore the unfamiliar town. He ended up staying in Effingham and managed to land a job fitting pipes together for a heating system being installed in a hotel near the train station.

One of the hotel guests was James Hill, who managed a 50,000-acre farm near Hallock, Minnesota. When the hotelkeeper heard that Hill was looking for a mechanic to keep his machinery in good condition, he recommended that Hill talk with Fred Jones. Jones accepted the new challenge offered by Hill, and on a snowy Christmas Day in 1912, he arrived in Hallock, Minnesota, his home for the next 18 years.

Steam engines, gasoline-driven tractors, hay loaders, cream separators, ditching and fencing machines, road graders, and harvesters—all this machinery and more was on the farm for Jones to work on. Hill also had several cars that had to be kept in good running order. There was plenty of work for the new mechanic to do and plenty of opportunity for him to learn.

Fred turned every new problem into a learning situation. After the sun went down, he spent his time reading books on electricity, engines, and other subjects, adding to his knowledge of mechanical engineering. Jones did more than just work and study. In Hallock, he made many friends with whom he hunted and fished. He sang in the town quartet and played the saxophone in the town band.

During World War I, Frederick Jones enlisted in the Army. He served in France as an electrician and earned the rank of sergeant. When the war ended, he returned to Hallock and became employed at a garage where cars, tractors, and farm machinery were repaired. He liked complicated jobs and would often make different parts out of the scraps and pieces of old machinery.

Jones' new employer, Oscar Younggren, was a racing car "bug," and together they toured the dirt-track circuit. They whipped up a racer from a Dodge frame and engine, installed Hudson "super-six" valves, a Ford Model-T rear axle, and an oil pump from a Rumley tractor. Jones raced for a number of years and set several track records at county fairground events.

One day in 1925, Jones was scheduled for a five-mile race. Three racers had already been killed in accidents that day at the track. Jones was nervous, and once into his race he hit a turn at 100 miles per hour, sliding into a fence and clipping several posts before his car rolled to a stop. He was knocked unconscious. When Jones came to, he found himself in an ambulance. His injuries were not severe, but that day ended Jones' racing career.

Going to the Movies

Fred Jones' imagination and ability led him to other adventures. The first radios were beginning to come to Minnesota, and Jones soon found himself surrounded with coils, tubes, and condensers. He bought books on electronics and on acoustics (the science of sound), and his self-education continued. When the publisher of the Hallock newspaper obtained a radiobroadcasting license, Fred Jones built the first transmitter for the station. He built many table model radios for his friends in Hallock so they could listen to the local station.

Jones also worked at the Grand Theater in Hallock, where he ran the movie projector. When "talking" movies became available, the theater owner realized that he would have to install sound equipment in order to continue to attract his customers. But he couldn't afford to buy the expensive equipment needed for sound films. So Jones offered to try to build some sound equipment himself.

Using some heavy steel disks from a plow, a leather machine belt, sprockets from an automobile piston, and some other odds and ends, Fred Jones built a soundtrack unit that was as good as anything that could have been purchased. His device, which kept sound records in time with the moving film, cost less than $100 to make. The commercial outfits available at the time cost about $3,000.

But by 1930 most good motion pictures were made with the soundtrack on the film itself. The records which once provided the sound for movies were on their way out.

With the soundtrack placed directly on the film, new equipment was necessary.

Again, Fred Jones decided to build his own device for combining sound with film. Using information he gained from reading—and his own creative ideas—Jones took a glass rod and ground it into the shape of a half cylinder. Then, by connecting the reshaped rod to a photoelectric cell, he was able to produce a narrow beam of light. When this beam of light hit the moving film, the movie soundtrack was made audible.

Within a short period of time, the Grand Theater in Hallock was in step with the modern "talking" movies. News of Fred Jones' work soon reached the ears of Joseph Numero in Minneapolis. Numero owned a company that manufactured motion picture equipment. He was having trouble constructing sound-pickup devices and decided to invite Jones to Minneapolis to help him.

Little did Numero realize that this invitation would result in the business of manufacturing refrigeration units for trucks and railway cars.

Fred Jones accepted Numero's job offer and joined Cinema Supplies in 1930. The sound equipment made by Numero's firm was used in movie houses throughout the northern Midwest.

On June 27, 1939, Frederick Jones received his first patent. He had invented a ticket dispensing machine for movie house tickets. This ex-racing car builder was now benefiting the motion picture business and contributing to the entertainment of thousands of Americans.

A Cool Idea

In the late 1930s, Fred Jones was still working as an engineer for Numero's firm. Instead of movie house equipment, however, he was busy designing portable air coolers for trucks that would carry perishable foods.

The switch from the movie house supply business to cold boxes occurred soon after Jones invented the first truck air conditioner. Numero sold his interests in theater equipment, and he and Jones devoted their full time to cold storage.

In 1949, the U.S. Thermo Control Company, founded jointly by Jones and Numero, had boomed to a $3-million-a-year business. The company manufactured automatic air coolers for trains, ships, and airplanes so foodstuffs could be kept fresh for long periods of time. And Jones was behind it all.

As an inventor, Frederick Jones was never satisfied with the improvements that he made in his cooling units. He developed ways to keep the air around the food at a constant temperature. He created devices that produced special atmospheric conditions to protect strawberries and other fruits from drying out or becoming too ripe before reaching the supermarkets. Other improvements regulated the moisture in the air and controlled air circulation.

Jones' inventions made it possible, for the first time, to transport meat, fruit, vegetables, eggs, butter, produce, and other perishable foods over long distances during any season of the year.

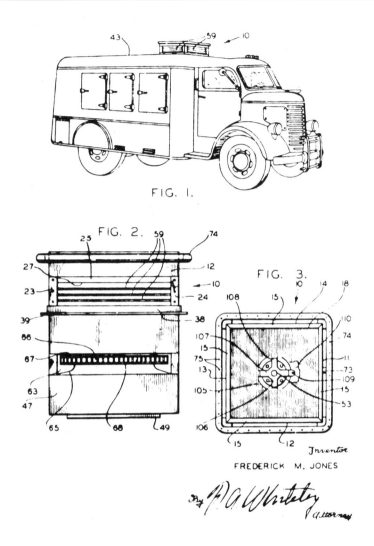

FIG. 1.

FIG. 2.

FIG. 3.

Inventor

FREDERICK M. JONES

By P. A. Whiteley
attorney

REMOVABLE COOLING DEVICE
Patented July 12, 1949

Jones' removable cooling device, Figures 2 and 3, helped trucks to carry perishable foods. Figure 1 shows how the device fit on a truck.

In his application to the Patent Office for a Removable Cooling Unit, Frederick Jones wrote the following:

My invention relates to a removable cooling unit for compartments of trucks, railroad cars and the like employed in transporting perishables and to a method of cooling such compartments and has for its object to provide a simple and compact self-contained cooling unit positioned at the top of said compartment and combined with air flow passages which produce a vortex of cold air flowing about the walls of the compartment and returning from the center of the compartment.

Perishables such as meats, vegetables, fruits, and the like are transported in what are known as refrigerator cars by rail and, to a greatly increased degree at the present time, in trucks. This transportation, taking place as it does over long routes which in the summertime are at high temperatures throughout and even in wintertime may be in part at high temperatures, requires artificial cooling in order to preserve said perishables in suitable condition for use as food.

In the case of refrigerator railroad cars, heavy cooling means, such as large ice compartments or large and heavy refrigerating plants, can be practically employed. This is not true of trucks where the necessary limitations of their use call for cooling means relatively low weight and so positioned as to take up as little as possible of the space within the transporting compartment.

It is a principle object of my invention, therefore, to provide a cooling unit small in size and weight, and positioned, together with the air-conducting passages, so as to occupy substantially none of the storage space within the vehicle compartment.

It is a further object of my invention to provide a unit which shall be mounted in the front wall of the compartment partly outside and partly inside and having its top adjacent to the top wall of the compartment.

With a few changes, Fred Jones' portable cooling units were important to the American military effort in World War II. He designed refrigerator units that were sent to Army hospitals and battlefields in the South Pacific. The units were needed to keep blood serum for transfusions and medicines at certain temperatures.

Army helicopters were used to transport the coolers to remote jungle outposts in the South Pacific islands. Other coolers were used on airplanes that flew wounded soldiers home over the Pacific. Some of these units could even produce heat if needed.

A Lifetime of Achievement

During his lifetime, Fred Jones was awarded more than 60 patents. Forty of these patents were for refrigeration equipment. Other patents were for such devices as portable X-ray machines and sound equipment techniques for motion pictures. Jones also patented many of the parts of his air cooling machines: the self-starting gasoline engine that turned his cooling units on and off, the reverse cycling mechanism for producing heat or cold, and devices for controlling air temperature and moisture.

At 50 years of age, Frederick Jones was one of the outstanding authorities in the field of refrigeration in the United States. In 1944, he was elected to membership in the American Society of Refrigeration Engineers. College-graduated scientists and engineers welcomed the chance to work with and learn from him. During the 1950s, he was called to Washington, D.C., to give advice on problems having to do with refrigeration. He was a consultant to the Defense Department and the Bureau of Standards.

By the time Frederick McKinley Jones passed away in Minneapolis in 1961, his inventions were serving people throughout the world. He was a major behind-the-scenes contributor to the quality of our lives today.

JAN E. MATZELIGER

4

Take off one of your shoes. Now, look at it carefully. Your shoe has three basic parts: sole, heel, and upper. The upper is the part that covers the top of your foot. Notice the shape of the different parts and how they are held together. It looks quite simple—just some sewing and a few nails. The history of this basic item of clothing is actually quite ancient, and at one time shoes were the product of many hours of hand labor.

For several thousand years, people have worn some form of foot covering. Shoes are so familiar to us that we accept them with very little thought. They are worn not only for their appearance but, more important, for the protection and comfort they give us.

One reason shoes are taken for granted is that we have so many of them. But this was not always so. Until about 100 years ago, there was no machinery for making shoes. The work was done completely by hand. The tools that were used for shoemaking—the knife, the awl, and the hammer—had changed little from the days of the early Egyptians. With these tools, a shoemaker did well if he made one pair a day. Consequently, shoes were scarce, expensive, and only the rich owned more than one pair.

When Thomas Beard, a London shoemaker, arrived in Salem, Massachusetts, in 1629, he became one of the first American shoemakers. Beard did quite a brisk business, and other European shoemakers followed him to America.

During the 1600s, skilled shoe craftsmen were scarce. Since the demand for shoes was great, America's pioneer shoemakers could charge high prices for their work. Then, unskilled workers started to make shoes for themselves and others at a lower cost. This competition hurt the business of the professional shoemakers.

So, in 1648, the shoemakers in and around Boston, Massachusetts, formed a union in order to protect their trade. They called this union the Company of Shoemakers. By the end of the 1600s, the union was turning out large quantities of shoes, still entirely handmade.

In the 1700s, colonial America's shoemaking center shifted to Lynn, Massachusetts, a small town near Boston. Shoes had been made there since 1630, and they were known for their high quality.

Throughout the 1770s, shoemakers and apprentices flocked to the town to learn their trade. Many considered it an honor to be trained by the Lynn craftsmen.

Today, of course, shoes are made by machines. The change from handmade shoes to machine-made ones was slow and gradual. Between 1850 and 1900, machinery gradually replaced hand labor. As a result, the little shops and businesses scattered throughout New England tended to disappear. They were replaced by large, power-driven, and machine-equipped factories.

One of these machines—the shoe lasting machine— was invented by Jan E. Matzeliger, an African American who worked in Lynn as a shoe machine mechanic. His machine replaced the only operation in the shoemaking process that was still being done by hand. Matzeliger's machine was an invention that changed the industry more than any other device.

During his lifetime, Jan Matzeliger saw his invention increase shoe production tenfold while also decreasing the hours of labor needed to make shoes. The lasting machine resulted in lower costs to both the shoe manufacturer and the customer.

Before we take a closer look at Matzeliger's ingenious invention, let's find out what the terms "last" and "lasting" really mean.

A Cobbler's Trade

The last is a reproduction of the approximate shape of the human foot. The last is made into a model of a customer's foot. A properly constructed shoe, when made over this form, will result in a shoe that supports and protects the foot without any pressure or binding. The last, therefore, is very important to the end result; the fitting, walking ease, and stylish appearance of a finished shoe all depend upon it.

The word "last" comes from the Anglo-Saxon word "laest," which means a footprint, foot-track, or foot-trace. In colonial days, when a person was having a pair of shoes made, he or she was not always around to try them on for size and fit, and so it was natural that some sort of form should be made on which to shape the shoe. It was equally natural to call this form by the word that meant a footprint or a foot-track.

Today, our shoes are still built on lasts. Lasts are made in many sizes by a machine. In the factory, they become the molds upon which the parts of the upper are formed. They are the foundation of shoemaking, determining the size, shape, and fit of all footwear.

When Thomas Beard and other pioneer shoemakers came to America, their shoemaking kits contained only the simplest of tools. Apparently, Beard brought no lasts with him for there is a mention that he "whittled his lasts from hard maple or hard wood." (Ancient shoe craftsmen made their shoes over lasts chiseled out of stone.)

Real progress in the history of shoemaking began in 1846 with the invention of the sewing machine by Elias Howe. Shortly thereafter, the Howe sewing machine was adapted to sew the various parts of a shoe together. During the next 17 years, many changes were made, and different machines were developed to make shoes. However, no one designed a machine to sew the upper to the sole.

Some inventors spent large amounts of money and time trying to invent a machine that would last shoes, but none of them met with success. It seemed that the lasting of shoes would always remain a hand process.

Because of this fact, the hand lasters became the ruling craftsmen of the shoe workers. They were skillful, and they earned high wages. Most of them were proud of their position in the trade and even boasted about it.

In Lynn, a laster voiced his opinion in these words: "No matter if the sewing machine is a wonderful machine. No man can build a machine that will last shoes and take away the job of the laster, unless he can make a machine that has fingers like a laster—and that is impossible."

That boast was heard by a young black mechanic who was operating a McKay sewing machine in a Lynn shoe factory in 1880. Jan Matzeliger was about to do what most people believed couldn't be done. He was about to do the impossible. Jan Matzeliger would design a machine that would shape the upper leather over the last and attach this leather to the sole of the shoe with tacks.

Since then, Jan Matzeliger's machine has been some-what changed and improved, but its principle remains the same. Today, in Lynn and other shoe manufacturing cities throughout the world, automatic lasters are in use.

On May 16, 1967, the city of Lynn, Massachusetts, honored its nineteenth-century inventor. Sponsored by the local branch of the National Association for the Advancement of Colored People (NAACP), the celebration was called Jan E. Matzeliger Day, and many citizens supported it. In the evening, a banquet was held in honor of Matzeliger. Jackie Robinson, the first African American to play major-league baseball, was the guest speaker.

A Foreigner Moves to Lynn

Matzeliger had come to Lynn some 90 years before the year in which he was honored. When he arrived in Lynn on a raw, chilly day back in the winter of 1877, he could barely speak the English language.

Jan Matzeliger was not born in America. He was born in Paramaribo, in the South American country of Surinam (Dutch Guiana), in 1852. His father was a Dutch engineer who had married a native black Surinamese woman. Her ancestors probably came from West Africa. Between 1650 and 1820, some 300,000 West Africans were brought to Dutch Guiana as enslaved people.

Matzeliger's father had been sent to Surinam by the Dutch government to direct the government machine work in the Dutch colony. At the age of 10, young Matzeliger went to work in the machine shops supervised by his father. He learned rapidly and showed a definite talent for fixing and operating machinery.

In 1871, at the age of 19, the tall, slender mechanic left his home to travel and learn more about the world. He spent two years as a sailor on an East Indian merchant ship. Then, in 1873, when his ship docked in Philadelphia, young Matzeliger decided to end his seafaring life. Though he couldn't speak a word of English, Matzeliger was a good mechanic, and he managed to find odd jobs, including one working with a cobbler.

Little is known about Matzeliger's life in Philadelphia, except that he probably became a devout Christian during his years in this city. He must have heard about the rapid growth of the shoe industry in Massachusetts for more than half of the shoes being produced in the entire country at the time were coming from Lynn. There was a constant demand for more workers, and people were moving to shoe centers like Lynn to fill job openings. Hoping for a better job, Matzeliger arrived in Lynn in 1877, alone and poor.

Since he was a black foreigner and spoke hardly any English, he had trouble getting a job. He went from factory to factory, only to be turned down each time. Shoe factory owners saw little use for his background and training. No one realized that his ambition and inventive mind would soon be vitally important to the shoe industry.

Matzeliger was a determined young man. Not easily discouraged, he learned to speak and write the English language. Eventually, he landed a job as an apprentice in a shoe factory, operating a McKay sole-sewing machine. After stitching shoes all day in the factory, he attended evening school to continue his study of English.

Because of his natural mechanical ability, Matzeliger became an important worker in the shoe factory. He took a special interest in the machine-driven operations that went on around him. As he did his daily sewing tasks, he often thought about the problems with the shoe machinery that was being used at the time.

Although his days were busy and long, Matzeliger still found time on weekends to drive a coach to and from a picnic park in West Lynn. He was gradually becoming settled in the town where he was to spend the remainder of his short life.

Wherever Matzeliger lived, he was known as modest, pleasant, and friendly. At a time when most Lynn people were inclined to look down on him because of his dark skin, he was still able to make a few close friends.

Matzeliger was a very religious man. In his coat lapel, he always wore a small medal that he had brought from Philadelphia. This medal was inscribed with the words "Safe in Jesus."

When he tried to attend white churches in Lynn, however, Matzeliger was turned away because he was black. But in 1884 he was welcomed by the Christian Endeavor Society, a young adult group at the North Congregational Church. Many of Matzeliger's church friends worked with him in the shoe factory.

Although Jan Matzeliger was never an official member of the North Congregational Church, he regularly attended its Sunday services. He even taught Sunday school classes for the society.

The "Last" Piece of the Puzzle

Matzeliger became more and more fascinated with machinery. Creative and industrious, he never stopped working and studying hard at his trade. He bought books on physics and mechanical science as well as his own drawing instruments and tools. He began to produce a variety of devices—an orange-wrapping machine, a railroad car coupler, and some shoe machinery parts.

Having little money, Matzeliger was unable to patent and manufacture his first inventions. One of them, the railroad car coupler, came into general use only after his employer put up the money for its development and manufacture. Later, the employer claimed the patent for the device in his own name.

Matzeliger, however, had another idea by now. He was thinking about a machine that could last shoes.

Labor conditions at the time increased Matzeliger's interest in a possible lasting machine. In 1877, the shoe lasters were organized into a union and were at the height of their power. They had frequent disputes with shoe manufacturers and often went on strike to force their employers to meet their demands for more pay or better working conditions. When this happened, other departments of the factory came to a standstill. Many workers were left idle.

The lasters felt they could do pretty much as they pleased since there was no machine to take their place. This attitude irritated Matzeliger. He felt it was unfair that he and many others would be without work and wages for periods of time. He said that he would put an end to the rule of the hand lasters by inventing a machine that would do their job perfectly. His fellow workers only jeered at him. They didn't realize that Matzeliger was serious about everything he attempted.

His problem was to design a successful machine that worked exactly like the hands of the skilled human laster. "I must carefully study the hands of a laster in action," he thought to himself, "and then recreate the movements of his hands with moving metal parts—gears, levers, and cams." So Matzeliger began to study the precise motions of the hand laster. He even got his job in the shoe factory changed so as to be near the lasting department.

It had not occurred to anyone else that this approach might bring success. Matzeliger started from scratch and worked alone. Consequently, he was not influenced by the ideas—and mistakes—of those who had tried before him.

Because there was still much opposition to machinery replacing people in the factories, Matzeliger decided that he would do his work secretly. The lasters' union was very powerful. Had the lasters known what he was doing, they probably would have had Matzeliger fired. He rented a room over the old West Lynn Mission. There, he could work at his sketches and experiment with models.

During the day, Jan Matzeliger would study the hand lasters at work. His keen eyes followed their exact finger movements, and he noted the way one hand operated in time with the other. Lasting was a job for strong hands.

It required constant pulling in a circular motion as the leather on the upper part of the shoe was tacked onto the insole. Matzeliger quietly watched this process hour after hour. When his day at the factory was over, he would return to his rented room and work far into the night.

He started out by making rough drawings of machine parts and how they fitted together. Each hand movement had to be imitated. Soon, a crude model began to take shape. Made of parts cut from old cigar boxes, pieces of wood, bits of wire, and nails, it performed the movements that were a necessary part of the lasting process. This first model took six months to build.

Despite his secrecy, word about what Matzeliger was doing in the room over the mission leaked out. When they saw his model, people laughed at what they called "the funny looking thing made from scraps of cardboard, wood, wire, and nails." Some people tried to warn Matzeliger how others had failed. Very few encouraged him.

Matzeliger needed money to continue his work but could find no one to support him. One man who had been trying to invent such a machine offered Matzeliger $50 for his first rough model. Matzeliger was ready to sell it, but he changed his mind at the last minute. This bit of interest by another inventor assured Matzeliger that he was on the right track.

He was determined to perfect his first attempt.

The second model had to be made of metal parts. Matzeliger began to collect bits of scrap metal and the discarded parts of old, broken-down machines. But now that he was going to work his idea into metal, he needed a machine shop in which to continue his experiment. He managed to acquire a small space in the factory where he was employed.

Each night, he worked away at his model—forging, filing, machining, and fitting. It was extremely hard work.

After four years of steady and lonely work, Matzeliger was a tired man. He was poor, too, since he had been using all of his earnings to build his machine. He often denied himself good meals, spending his daily wages on his invention rather than food. Often, he ate nothing but cornmeal mush.

Jan Matzeliger's patient and exhausting years of work resulted in an improved but still imperfect model. The lack of money was a real problem for him now that the model had been completed. Cash was needed to get a patent and to arrange for the completion of the machine so that it could be tried out in a factory.

Some offers came in to buy the rights to parts of the machine—$1,500 for the device that turned the leather around the toe of the shoe, for instance. With this offer, Jan Matzeliger was even more convinced that he had the beginnings of a great invention. He wanted investors who would back the whole machine.

Finally, he found two wealthy Lynn citizens willing to put up money. For their financing, the investors gained ownership of two-thirds of the invention. Jan Matzeliger set out to build an improved third model. When his third model was finished, Matzeliger applied for a patent.

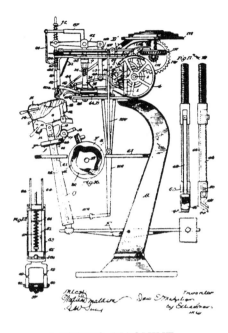

LASTING MACHINE
Patented March 20, 1883

Patents are usually granted on the basis of detailed drawings sent to the U.S. Patent Office in Washington, D.C. After studying Matzeliger's drawings, Patent Office officials could hardly believe that a machine could do what Matzeliger claimed his could do. A representative of the Patent Office came to Lynn to examine Matzeliger's model. Finally, in March 1883, Jan E. Matzeliger was awarded Patent No. 274,207 for his "Lasting Machine."

However, he was still not completely satisfied with his work. After testing his machine under factory conditions, he found that many improvements were still necessary. And so he worked for two more years on experiments and test runs. By the spring of 1885, he was ready to test a much improved machine. On May 29, his machine lasted 75 pairs of women's shoes perfectly. It passed the test.

A Sudden Success

Suddenly, Matzeliger had many friends. People with money to invest as well as companies already in the shoe machinery business wanted to exploit his invention and gain quick and huge profits. The outcome was the formation of the Consolidated Lasting Machine Company.

This company took over Jan Matzeliger's patents, for which he received a large block of stock in the company. The company immediately began rapid production of the new machine. The 225 workers building the Matzeliger lasters could hardly keep up with orders for the machine. Matzeliger's laster was on its way to revolutionizing shoe manufacturing.

An expert hand laster working 10 hours a day could produce about 50 pairs of shoes. Matzeliger's laster could turn out from 150 to 700 pairs each day depending on the quality of work. By 1889, the demand for the shoe lasting machine was overwhelming. The Lasting Machine Company set up a school in Lynn where hand lasters and others could learn how to operate the new machine.

The merits of Matzeliger's invention were recognized by shoe manufacturers as a boon to their business. But to the hand lasters, the machine was a threat. It broke the power of their union because unskilled workers at lower wages could be hired to operate the machine.

Naturally, the lasters opposed the machine. Its inventor was a black man, and the lasters scornfully called it the "Nigger Machine." They ridiculed it whenever possible.

One tale, often heard around Lynn in the early 1900s, was started by an old laster. The "Nigger Machine," so the story went, had human fingers, it worked with human intelligence, and it actually talked. The sounds coming from the machine when in operation seemed to echo the words: "I've got your job. I've got your job."

Remembering His Friends

Jan Matzeliger did not live to see the results of his hard work and creativity. Sadly, he never enjoyed the fame and fortune that he deserved. He had driven himself too hard. He was weak from the strain of overworking, often going without enough sleep and food. Sunday had been his only day of relaxation, when he attended church and taught Sunday school.

On a chilly, wet day in 1886, Jan Matzeliger caught a cold. The cold lingered on and developed into something more serious. He became bedridden. Matzeliger's condition became worse, and he moved from his room over the mission to a home where friends could care for him.

Finally, Matzeliger's illness was diagnosed as tuberculosis. A doctor ordered him to the Lynn Hospital, where he was to spend his last days. On August 24, 1889, when he was only 37 years old, Jan E. Matzeliger died.

Four months before his death, Matzeliger made out his will. In it, he remembered everyone who had been close to him. To 15 of his friends, his hospital doctor, and Lynn Hospital, he left blocks of company stock. To others, he left his gold watch and chain, the paintings done during his years of illness, his Bibles, and the instruments that he used to sketch the designs of his invention.

The greatest beneficiary in Matzeliger's will was the North Congregational Church of Lynn. When other church groups had rejected him upon his arrival in Lynn, it was the North Church that befriended him. To this church, he left the bulk of his stock.

In 1904, the North Church sold part of the stock that Matzeliger had willed to it for $10,000. This money made it possible for the church to pay off all of its mortgages. Years later, the North Church merged with another Lynn church to become the First Church of Christ.

In the First Church of Christ, at the morning services on Sunday, September 8, 1968, remembrance was given to Jan Matzeliger. The church bulletin that the parishioners received that morning contained the following:

> We are taking a few minutes this morning to honor the life of Jan Ernst Matzeliger. Jan Matzeliger's invention of the shoe lasting machine was perhaps the most important invention for New England. His invention was the greatest forward step in the shoe industry. Yet, because of the color of his skin, he was not mentioned in the major history books of the United States. . . .
>
> It was the sales of some more of his stocks which helped to make it possible to have this present church. We are not honoring Matzeliger because he gave the church money, but because he is a hero with whom the American people can identify.

On September 15, 1991, the Postal Service issued a twenty-nine cent stamp honoring Jan Matzeliger. On a rainy fall afternoon, more than 200 people attended the ceremony for the release of the stamp. The stamp, the fourteenth in the Postal Service's Black Heritage Series, brought long-overdue recognition to an African American of indomitable spirit, a man who set and achieved what seemed to be an impossible goal. More than a hundred years after Jan Matzeliger's death, his adopted country paid a fitting tribute to a man who left his "stamp" on the story of America.

LEWIS H. LATIMER

5

*"I was one of the pioneers of the electric
lighting industry from its creation until it had
become worldwide in its influence."*

This statement was made by Lewis Latimer. Not only
was he an inventor who worked with Thomas
Edison, the creator of the first practical electric light bulb,
but Latimer also drew the plans for Alexander Graham
Bell's first telephone patent.

Lewis H. Latimer was the only African-American
member of the Edison Pioneers, a group of distinguished
scientists and inventors who worked for Thomas Edison.
Edison used a teamwork approach in solving scientific and

technological problems. His laboratory in Menlo Park and West Orange, New Jersey, became a model for the huge industrial research centers that have become so important in twentieth-century American life. The team approach to scientific discovery and technology is widely used today.

Edison's most important invention was the incandescent light bulb. As an inventor of certain light bulb parts and a valuable member of Edison's team, Lewis Latimer helped to make the Edison lighting system possible.

When Latimer died in December 1928, the Edison Pioneers released a statement to the press about his life and his contributions to the field of electric lighting. Part of the press release read as follows:

> Mr. Latimer successfully produced a method of making carbon filaments for the Maxim electric incandescent lamp, which he patented. His keen perception of the possibility of the electric light and kindred industries resulted in his being the author of several other inventions. . . . In 1884, he became associated with the engineering department of the Edison Electric Light Company. . . . He was of the colored race, the only one in our organization, and was one of those to respond to the initial call that led to the formation of the Edison Pioneers, on January 24, 1918. Broadmindedness, versatility in the accomplishment of things intellectual and cultural, a linguist, a devoted husband and father—all were characteristic of him, and his genial presence will be missed from our gatherings.

Boston Boyhood

During the 1800s, tens of thousands of black people escaped from slavery in the South by fleeing to northern states. George Latimer was one such slave. He escaped from Virginia to gain his freedom and to start a new life in Boston, Massachusetts. There, George Latimer met and married another fugitive slave from Virginia. They had four children, three boys and a girl. Lewis H. Latimer, born in September 1848, was the youngest of the family.

From his boyhood background, it is rather unlikely that anyone would have predicted fame for the youngest son of two fugitive slaves. While Lewis Latimer attended elementary school in Boston, he also worked a few hours each day in his father's barbershop.

Later, when his father became a paperhanger, young Lewis worked with him at night and became quite expert at paperhanging. At the age of 10, he left school and began working full-time helping his father.

Then, for some unknown reason, George Latimer left home, deserting his wife and four children. Lewis' mother was unable to support her children. Mrs. Latimer sent her daughter to live with a friend and her two oldest sons to a farm school in the western part of Massachusetts. Lewis remained in his mother's home until she got a chance to go to sea as a ship's stewardess. Then, he was sent to the same school as his brothers. (They were no longer there, though one of them was working nearby.)

Lewis remained at the farm school for several years until one day when his brother William returned for a visit. William was surprised to find his brother at the school and suggested that they run away and return to their native Boston. This appealed to Lewis since he longed to be free of the farm chores he had to do at school. He wanted to find a job where he could use his mind instead of his muscles.

Boston was more than 80 miles away. Lewis and his brother planned their escape carefully, fearing that along the way they might be chased and caught by the school authorities. Running, walking, stealing rides on the railway, and begging for food along the way, Lewis and his brother arrived in Boston several days after fleeing from the farm school. Perhaps now Lewis knew how his mother and father felt when they escaped from slavery.

The Making of a Draftsman

Back in Boston, and only 13 years old, Lewis moved from one odd job to another. He worked first as an office boy in a law firm and later waited tables in the home of a wealthy family.

In 1863, soon after the Civil War began, Lewis Latimer was 15 years old. He was tired of Boston and working at odd jobs. Both of his brothers had joined the Navy, so Lewis, pretending to be older than he was, also enlisted. He served as a cabin boy. At the end of the war in 1865, Latimer was honorably discharged from the U.S. Navy and returned to Boston.

After many weeks of trying to find work, Lewis finally secured a position as an office assistant with the firm of Crosby and Gould, Patent Solicitors. His pay was three dollars a week. He worked in a large room filled with drafting tables. There, leaning over the tables for hours, men made detailed drawings of inventions.

The work of the patent draftsmen fascinated Lewis Latimer. As he watched them making drawings of inventions for the U.S. Patent Office, he noted what books they used. Later, at a secondhand bookstore, Lewis purchased some books that gave drawing instructions. Then, with more of his savings, he was able to buy a set of drawing instruments. Each day, as he moved around the office, Lewis Latimer looked over the draftsmen's shoulders to see how they used their tools.

In the evening, he practiced and practiced, making drawings like those of the professional draftsmen he saw during the day. Lewis was determined to be as good as they were.

Arriving at work one morning, young Latimer asked one of the draftsmen if he could do some drawing for him. At first, the draftsman laughed, but then he decided to see what the office boy could do at the drawing board. He handed Lewis a piece of drawing paper and left him alone with an assignment. When the draftsman returned, he was surprised to see how well the young man could draw. So, from time to time, he let Lewis do some of the work.

One day, Lewis' boss saw him at the drawing board and was so pleased with his work that he promoted Lewis from office assistant to junior draftsman.

Lewis began drawing eight hours a day. Often, he made working models of inventions to go along with the drawings required by the Patent Office.

Lewis Latimer stayed with Crosby and Gould for 11 years. When he left, he was making $80 a week.

In 1876, Alexander Graham Bell applied for a U.S. patent on his telephone invention. Bell was teaching sign language to deaf people in Boston, and his school was near the offices of Crosby and Gould. Bell came to the office to have his patent drawings made, and Latimer was assigned to draw his telephone system. Latimer carefully noted the instructions he received from the great inventor "as to how I was to make the drawings for the application for a patent upon the telephone."

At 30 years of age, Lewis Latimer had become a skilled and respected draftsman of patents. He knew a great deal about the science of invention for he had an active and creative mind.

Latimer wasn't satisfied with his accomplishments, however. He wanted to do more. Lewis Latimer believed that many of the inventions that he had so carefully drawn could be improved upon.

Lewis Latimer's dream was to become an inventor.

Bright Ideas

In the year 1879, Latimer left Boston and went to Bridgeport, Connecticut, to live with his married sister. His first job was in a machine shop. There, Latimer was assigned the task of making mechanical drawings.

When Hiram Maxim, inventor of the machine gun, entered the machine shop one day, he was surprised to see a draftsman who was black—and to see the fine drawings that Lewis Latimer was making. At the time, Maxim was chief engineer of the United States Electrical Lighting

Company. He had been looking for a qualified draftsman to do patent drawings, and he soon realized that Latimer was his man.

While working for Maxim as a mechanical draftsman and secretary, Latimer learned everything he could about electric light construction and operation. In 1879, Thomas Edison invented an electric light, and Latimer began to experiment with ways to improve Edison's lamp.

In 1880, when Maxim moved his company to New York City, Lewis Latimer moved with him.

When he wasn't drawing, Latimer was put in charge of producing the carbon filaments for electric lamps. The filament is the material in a light bulb that glows when an electric current passes through it. For about 26 years, all light bulbs (incandescent lamps) had carbon filaments. They were made by burning the cellulose found in paper, bamboo, or cotton thread.

Cellulose is composed largely of carbon combined with some other elements, usually hydrogen and oxygen. When cellulose is heated in a closed furnace without air, it breaks down—the hydrogen, oxygen, and some of the carbon is driven off. Only a carbon skeleton remains. This skeleton, which is very hard and dense (like coal), became the filament material for the electric lamp.

In an incandescent lamp, the electric current heats to an almost white heat. This heat gives off the light we see. The hotter the filament is heated, the more light it radiates. The hotter the filament is heated, however, the sooner it wears out.

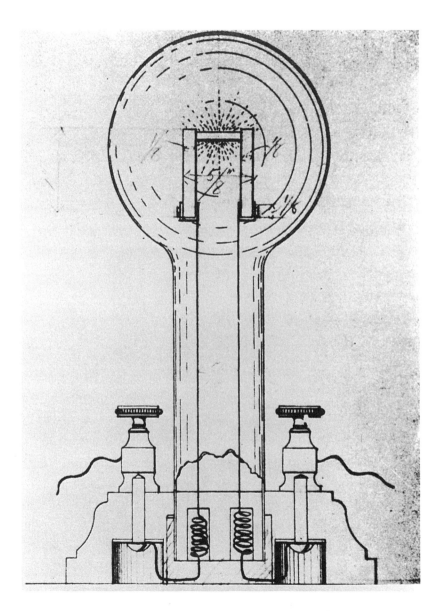

This sketch was used by Latimer as a model for the first technical drawing that he made for Hiram Maxim in 1880.

Thomas Edison felt that a good filament should last about 600 hours. But for Lewis Latimer, a good filament simply wasn't good enough.

Latimer worked very hard to improve the quality of the filament material. Gradually, the operating temperature of the bulb was raised without any loss to the life of the filament.

Lewis Latimer had successfully produced a method for making an improved and cheaper carbon filament for Maxim's electric lamp. This filament made it possible to operate lights safely at a high temperature. It also enabled more people to install them and to have electric lighting. In January 1882, Latimer received a patent on his electric light filament.

It wasn't long before this young black inventor was made the chief electrical engineer for Maxim's company. Latimer assisted in installing some of the first "Maxim" incandescent electric light plants in cities in the United States and Canada. At the same time, he supervised the production of carbon filaments made by his own process. His lamps lit the railroad stations in Montreal and New York City.

Later, Latimer was sent to London, England, where he established an incandescent lamp factory for Maxim's company. There, he instructed workmen in every aspect of making light bulbs, including the art of blowing glass.

Returning to the United States a year later, Latimer worked for two other companies. Shortly after his return, he designed and manufactured a lamp that bears his name and can be found in a famous collection of incandescent lamps at the Henry Ford Museum in Dearborn, Michigan. The Latimer Lamp is one of 800 lamps in the collection. Nearly all of them are early examples of the development of electric lighting systems.

In the year 1884, Latimer received an important call from Thomas Edison's company. He was offered a job as a draftsman at the Edison offices in New York City. This was the beginning of Lewis Latimer's long association with Thomas Edison.

Lewis Latimer became a draftsman in the legal department and remained there for 30 years. In Latimer's time, as today, inventors must protect their patented inventions from being stolen and manufactured by others for profit. Some men claimed that they had developed lamps similar to Edison's—and had done so earlier. They organized companies and produced lamps according to the principles in Edison's patents.

The legal department of Edison's company was set up to protect his many electrical inventions. Sometimes, a court case would result over who had rights to a certain invention. Latimer often made drawings for court exhibits. He traveled around the country inspecting patents and gathering information on people who tried to use inventions that belonged to the Edison company.

These court cases were often long legal battles. Many times Latimer was the star witness. Edison usually won his cases, and Latimer's knowledge of electrical patents was responsible for many of the victories.

Lewis Latimer was a great admirer of Thomas Edison and his work. He wanted everyone to know about electric lighting. In 1890, Latimer wrote the first book on electric lighting. His book, entitled *Incandescent Electric Lighting*, was a practical description of the Edison system.

In his book, Latimer described how light is produced by heating a filament to incandescence. After discussing the various parts of the electric light, he explained the operation of the incandescent light bulb:

> If the electric current can be forced through a substance that is a poor conductor, it will create a degree of heat in that substance, which will be greater or less according to the quality of electricity forced through it.
>
> Upon this principle of the heating effect of the electrical current is based the operation of the incandescent lamp just described. While copper and platinum wires readily conduct the current, the carbon filament offers a great deal of resistance to its passage and for this reason becomes very hot—in fact, is raised to white heat or incandescence, which gives its name to the lamp.
>
> You doubtless wonder why this thread of charcoal is not immediately consumed when in this state, but this is accounted for when you remember that without oxygen of the air, there can be no combustion, and that every possible trace of air has been removed from the bulb [which] is so thoroughly sealed up as to prevent admission of the air about it.
>
> And yet the lamp does not last forever, for the reason that the action of the current upon the carbon has a tendency to divide up its particles and transfer them from one point to another so that, sooner or later, the filament gives way at some point. Yet most of these lamps are guaranteed to last a thousand hours, and this—at from four to six hours a day—gives the lamp a life of several months.

A Different Kind of Light

Lewis Latimer did more than just help to bring electric light to the streets of New York, office buildings, homes, subway stations, and railroad cars. Through his many activities and interests, he brought "light" to the lives of those around him. Latimer worked hard for civil rights organizations. He taught immigrants the English language in a New York City community center.

Lewis Latimer expressed himself in other ways, too. When he had time, Latimer painted and wrote music and poetry. One of his poems—titled "Keep in Touch with the World"—provides a unique look at Lewis Latimer:

Keep in Touch with the World

Keep in touch with the world;
The days that are ours,
Are fleeting and soon
The night will be here.
If we've loved we have lived,
Midst its weeds and its flowers,
Midst its smiles and its laughter
As well as its tear.

Chorus

Keep in touch with the world;
With its joys and its sorrows.
Keep in touch with the world;
With its pleasure and pain;
With its crime and its care,
For who knows but tomorrow
We may leave it to never
Return here again.

Those only who suffer,
Can feel for each other.
Experience is teaching
As naught else can teach.
Each woman's our sister.
Each man is our brother.
To tell of our love,
Is the purpose of speech.

Chorus

Keep in touch with the world;
From the babe with its mother
To the tottering man
Deep wrinkled and gray.
To love while we live
And give aid to each other
Is the sunshine of life
That turns night into day.

ELIJAH MCCOY

6

Have you ever wondered where the saying "It's the real McCoy" comes from? And how it came to be part of our language? Its origin can be traced back to an African American who was a mechanic in the early 1870s. His name was Elijah McCoy.

As a young man, Elijah McCoy was fascinated with steam engines, and he began experimenting with them. During this period of history, most machines had to be stopped every time they needed oiling. Furthermore, the lubrication was done by hand oilers. Stopping and starting engines to oil them wasted a lot of time. It was also very expensive. McCoy realized that somehow a way had to be found to provide a continuous flow of oil to the moving parts of a machine while it was still operating.

It was Elijah McCoy who developed a small cup with a valve mechanism that could supply oil, drop by drop, to the moving parts of machines. This valve, called a stop-cock, finally made it possible to eliminate costly and time-consuming stoppages for lubrication.

McCoy's cup was extensively used on the engines and locomotives of the great western railways, on the steam-ships that crossed the Great Lakes, on transatlantic ocean liners, and on machinery in factories. No piece of heavy machinery was considered to be complete unless it was equipped with the McCoy lubricator.

And, eventually, railroad and factory inspectors, when checking out a new piece of machinery, began to ask, "Is it the real McCoy?" The phrase soon caught on. It was understood to mean "the real thing." It wasn't long before many people began to apply the expression to other things besides machinery.

McCoy lived most of his life in the city of Detroit, Michigan. Anyone who lived there between 1882 and 1929 had heard something about McCoy, but there were few people who knew him well. Occasionally, in answer to a question about McCoy, one would say, "He's the one that invented some kind of lubricator, isn't he?" Beyond this, most people knew very little or nothing about him.

Finding a Better Way

Elijah McCoy was born in May 1843, in Colchester, Ontario, in Canada. Both of his parents, who had been enslaved in Kentucky, escaped to Canada in the fall of 1837 via the Underground Railroad. (The Underground Railroad was the network of homes and farms where anti-slavery people hid escaping slaves and helped them on their way to freedom in the North.)

After settling in Canada, McCoy's father joined the Canadian army. Upon his honorable discharge, he was given 160 acres of farmland in Colchester. Elijah attended school and worked on his father's farm until he was 15 years old.

After his fifteenth birthday, McCoy's father sent him to Edinburgh, Scotland, to study mechanical engineering. After five years in Scotland, McCoy returned to Canada as a master mechanic and engineer. He worked there for a year and then left for the United States.

The best job that McCoy could find was that of a railroad fireman (a person who tends, or stokes, a train's fire). A bit discouraged, he began work on the Michigan Central Railroad.

At this time, wood was used as fuel to power steam locomotives. Men stood on the running board to pour oil from cups onto the steam chest of the engine. McCoy felt that there had to be a better way to lubricate these machines. His mechanical creativity and training started to work.

Around 1870, Elijah McCoy was living in Ypsilanti, Michigan, where he began experimenting in his machine shop with lubricators for steam engines. After two years of labor, on June 23, 1872, he received his first patent for a locomotive lubricator.

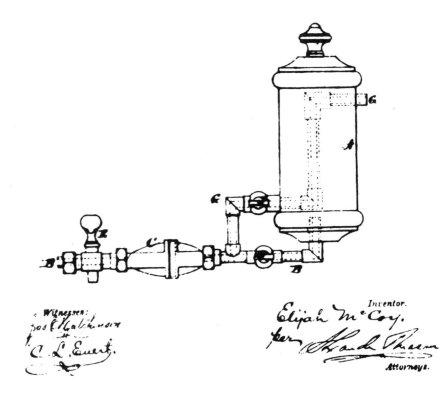

IMPROVEMENT IN LUBRICATORS
FOR STEAM ENGINES
Patented 1872

Elijah McCoy patented a new method of lubricating steam engines. His description of the invention appears on page 99.

In his letter of application to the U.S. Patent Office for a patent on one of his first lubricators, McCoy wrote the following description of his device:

To all whom it may concern:

Be it known that I, Elijah McCoy, of Ypsilanti, in the county of Washtenaw and in the State of Michigan, have invented certain new and useful Improvements in a Lubricator for Cylinders; and do hereby declare that the following is a full, clear, and exact description thereof, reference being had to the accompanying drawing and to the letters of reference marked thereon, making a part of the specification. . . .

A represents the vessel in which oil is contained, and from the bottom of which a pipe, B, leads to the steam-chest. This pipe is, at a suitable point, provided with a globe or reservoir, C. Between the vessel A and the globe or reservoir C is a stop-cock, D, in the pipe B, and in the same pipe, between the globe and the steamchest, is another stop-cock, E. A steampipe, G, passes from the dome or boiler down through the vessel and connects with the oil-pipe B at the glove or reservoir C, or at any point between the same and the valve D. In the steam-pipe G, after it leaves the vessel A, is a stop-cock, J. One of these oilers is to be placed on each side of the smoke-arch directly opposite the cylinder, and the various stop-cocks should be so connected with levers or rods that they can be operated simultaneously by a single rod in the engineer's cab. When the engine is working, the stop-cocks E and J are closed and the stop-cock D opened, allowing the oil to pass into the globe or reservoir C. The steam being in the pipe G prevents the oil from congealing in cold weather in the vessel A. When the cylinder is to be oiled, the stopcocks E and J are opened and D closed. Steam passing from the boiler or dome through the pipe G forces the oil out of the globe or reservoir C into the cylinder.

Elijah McCoy was not satisfied with his first attempt to develop a locomotive lubricator. He wanted to perfect his ideas, and in the next few years, McCoy obtained six patents for different types of machine lubricators. During his lifetime, he received a total of 57 patents.

At first, locomotive engineers were reluctant to use McCoy's new invention on their engines. They objected to the device because it had been invented by a black man. Some of the men taunted McCoy and called his lubricator a "nigger oilcup."

Despite objections, however, the oilcup was installed on many locomotives, often under the direct supervision of McCoy himself. It was not unusual for the engineers to be instructed by him on how to use it. From 1872 to 1915, most of the railroad locomotives in the United States, and many in foreign countries as well, were equipped with Elijah McCoy's lubricators.

"The Best Thing in the World"

From 1882 to 1926, 45 patents were awarded to Elijah McCoy. All but eight of them pertained to lubricating devices.

McCoy considered his Graphite Lubricator, patented in April 1915, to be his best invention. About 1920, he organized the Elijah McCoy Manufacturing Company, in Detroit, Michigan, to manufacture and sell this lubricator. It was designed to overcome the difficulties in oiling a kind of engine called a superheater. This engine operated by using large amounts of steam.

Before McCoy developed his Graphite Lubricator, the problems of lubricating the superheater engine were made clear by a Mr. Kelly in an article in the *Engineer's Journal.* Mr. Kelly wrote:

There is Need of a Remedy

There is no denying the fact that our present experience in lubricating the cylinders of engines using superheated steam is anything but satisfactory. Locomotive Superintendents and Master Mechanics are trying to make each other and everyone else believe that they have solved the problem, but perfect lubrication cannot be had unless there is provision made to supply the oil to cylinder with some degree of regularity. . . . If the oil feed was made regular so the steam would distribute it over the bearing surface of cylinder when the engine is working, these bearing surfaces would be better protected than is otherwise possible.

Our trouble from trying to lubricate cylinders of superheated engines is not so much due to a lack of an oil to withstand the heat of cylinders as to a lack of some way to supply the oil we have with some regularity while the engine is working.

McCoy's new lubricator used a solid substance called graphite as the lubricant. Graphite is a form of the element carbon and is the basic substance found in the lead of an ordinary pencil.

If you were to rub some powdered graphite between your fingers, you would find that it is soft, smooth, and greasy. Because of these properties, graphite makes an ideal lubricant. Perhaps you have lubricated bicycle parts or locks with this powdered material. Sometimes, it is mixed with oil or water, as it was in McCoy's lubricator.

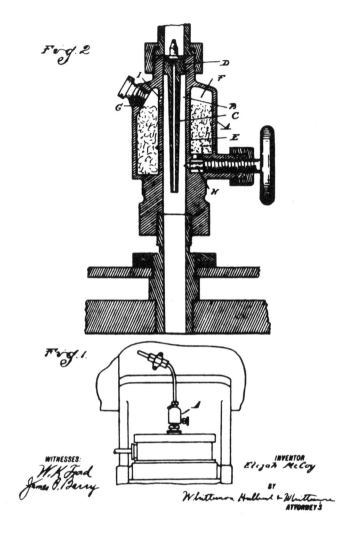

LOCOMOTIVE LUBRICATOR
Patented 1915

McCoy invented the Graphite Lubricator for use on railroad locomotives with superheater engines. This device provided a continuous flow of oil without clogging the engine.

In his letter of application for a patent, McCoy carefully described the mechanics of his Graphite Lubricator. McCoy's lubricator effectively met the problem of providing a continuous flow of oil to superheater engines:

To all whom it may concern:

Be it known that I, Elijah McCoy, a citizen of the United States of America, residing in Detroit, in the county of Wayne and State of Michigan, have invented certain new and useful Improvements in Locomotive-Lubricators, of which the following is a specification, reference being had therein to the accompanying drawings.

The invention relates to locomotive lubricators, and it is the particular object of the invention to provide means for introduction of graphite or other suspended solid lubricant without danger of clogging.

In the drawing: Figure 1 is an elevation of my improved lubricator, showing it as applied to a locomotive; and fig. 2 is a longitudinal section thereof.

In the present state of the art, locomotive lubricators are usually provided with a restricted passage, or choke-plug, which is arranged adjacent to the steam chest at the lower end of the oil conduit. This choke-plug is usually a separate fitting which has a screw-threaded engagement with the nipple entering the steam chest and a union coupling with the oil conduit. This is adapted for the feeding of a free-flowing oil, but a heavy lubricant and particularly one containing a suspended solid matter, such as graphite, is liable to obstruct the choke-plug so as to render the device inoperative.

With my improved construction, means is provided for feeding the heavy lubricant without danger of obstructing this choke-plug, this consisting essentially of a lubricant cup associated with a choke-plug, but so as not to clog the restricted passage.

The Graphite Lubricator met with a very enthusiastic reception from locomotive engineers. The superintendent of one large railroad wrote:

> We have found the Graphite Lubricator of considerable assistance in the lubrication of locomotives equipped with superheaters. . . . There is a decided advantage in better lubrication and reduction in wear in valves and piston rings, and as a well lubricated engine is more economical in the use of fuel, there is unquestionably a saving in fuel.

The master mechanic of a well-known Canadian railroad company agreed with this endorsement of the McCoy Graphite Lubricator: "It is the best thing in the world, as it saves us a world of trouble."

The Real McCoy

By 1923, Elijah McCoy was well known throughout the world for his mechanical genius. His inventions carried patents in many foreign countries—Great Britain, France, Germany, Austria, and Russia, to name just a few. He was often called upon as a consultant to give advice to large industrial concerns.

McCoy was also well known among the young people of Detroit, where he counseled teen-age boys. He believed that what he had accomplished, thousands of others could do if only they would apply themselves.

At 80 years of age, McCoy stood perfectly erect and was remarkably active. He was proud of his inventions. He was also proud of the fact that he could still touch his toes without bending his knees. But after 1926 McCoy's health began to fail. He was alone during his last days, his wife having died a few years earlier. In 1928, he was admitted to Eloise Infirmary in Eloise, Michigan, where he died in 1929.

Elijah McCoy's accomplishments as an inventor came during very difficult times for African Americans. When no positions were open to him despite the fact that he was a trained engineer, he took the nearest job to an engineer that he could get, that of a railroad fireman, and made the best of his opportunity.

The result was that Elijah McCoy became a teacher of engineers and a master among master mechanics. Daily papers and mechanical and engineering journals spoke highly of his work. His patents were used internationally, and his inventions contributed to the growth of our nation.

Elijah McCoy was as real as his work.

NORBERT RILLIEUX

7

It has been estimated that each person in the United States uses about 100 pounds of sugar a year. Like many of the things that you use each day, you probably take sugar for granted. Yet today it is one of our most common foods.

However, until fairly recently, sugar was a luxury. Few people could afford it, and for those who could, it was hard to get. The manufacturing process that changed the juice from the sugar cane plant into crystals of sugar was slow and expensive.

During the 1800s and early 1900s, many books and articles were written about the history of sugar manufacturing and refining. If you were to look at some of these, the name Rillieux would often appear. In 1846, Norbert Rillieux received a U.S. patent for an invention first used in a sugar factory near New Orleans, Louisiana. Rillieux had found a new way of turning sugar juice into a fine grade of white sugar crystals. The device was known as the multiple-effect vacuum evaporator.

Rillieux's evaporator greatly reduced production costs and provided a superior grade of sugar. Sugar producers proclaimed his invention as a revolution in the processing of raw sugar. Rillieux's method was quickly adopted by many sugar refineries.

Most historians who write about the development of the sugar industry are generous in their praise of Norbert Rillieux's contribution. But they often fail to mention that Rillieux was an African American.

J. G. McIntosh, in his book entitled *Technology of Sugar* (1903), devotes five pages to the development of Rillieux's evaporator. "This is a system which constitutes the basis of all the saving in fuel hitherto effected in sugar factories," McIntosh writes. "Rillieux may, therefore, with all justice, be regarded as one of the greatest benefactors of the sugar industry."

Another authority on the history of sugar, Charles A. Browne, a chemist with the U.S. Department of Agriculture, confirms the importance of Rillieux's contribution: "I have always held that Rillieux's invention is the greatest in the history of American chemical engineering. I know of no other invention that has brought as great a saving to all branches of chemical engineering."

Rillieux's invention was used throughout the sugar industry and also in the manufacturing of condensed milk, soap, gelatin, and glue. The idea underlying his device has not changed much since Rillieux first designed his system in the 1840s.

A Sweet Story

It should be made clear that sugar does not actually come from a sugar factory. It is made by green plants. A plant's green leaves, using the energy of sunlight, make sugar from water taken from the soil and carbon dioxide from the air. This process is called photosynthesis. (The term means "manufactured by light.")

Table sugar—or sucrose, as it is called by scientists— is the most famous of the many natural plant substances called sugars. The substance you use on your food has the same chemical make-up as the one naturally made in the sugar cane plant.

Sucrose can be removed in usable amounts from a number of plants. Some of these plants, like the sugar cane and the sugar beet, produce sugar more abundantly than others. They are the main commercial sources of sugar production.

Sugar cane is a giant grass-like plant. It grows in a warm, moist climate and stores sugar in its long stalk. At harvest time, the sugar cane is cut off near the ground.

The long stalks are stripped of their leaves and chopped into short lengths. The chopped stalks are then shipped to a raw sugar mill. During Rillieux's time, the stalks were taken to a mill located on a sugar plantation.

At the mill, the stalks are shredded by passing them through crushing rollers. This prepares the stalk fibers for grinding. The shredded cane is next fed through a series of heavy rollers that revolve against each other under great pressure. This action squeezes out the sugar cane juice, which is caught in pans below the rollers.

The cane juice is now ready to be changed into raw sugar. It is first treated to remove impurities. Then, it is boiled until it thickens and crystals form in it. The boiling evaporates water from the juice. The result is a mixture of molasses and sugar crystals.

A machine called a centrifuge spins the molasses and sugar around at a high speed, separating the sugar crystals from the molasses. Freed from the molasses, the sticky raw sugar is light brown in color. Further refining produces the clear, white sugar bought in a store.

At a refinery, the raw sugar is dissolved in warm water. This water-sugar solution is treated a number of times to remove other impurities and coloring. In order to have pure sugar crystals, almost all of the water must be removed or evaporated.

This is where Norbert Rillieux's invention came into the picture. About 1830, Rillieux began to study the problems of evaporating the water from the sugar juice in such a way that the sugar would crystallize.

Until the time of Rillieux's invention, enormous amounts of heat were needed to evaporate the water. This required burning large amounts of fuel, a process that was extremely expensive. Furthermore, much of the heat was wasted in this very slow procedure. Rillieux's method of evaporation involved a new way of using steam heat, a way that speeded up sugar production and cut the cost.

To France and Back

Norbert Rillieux's life was a complicated one, and not every detail is known. He was born on a plantation in New Orleans, Louisiana. Yet it was in France that he attended school and spent most of his lifetime.

Rillieux was born in March 1806. His father, Vincent Rillieux, a white Frenchman, was an engineer and master of the plantation on which Norbert's mother had been a slave. Since Rillieux's birth record indicates that he was born free, his mother must have been freed from slavery at some time before his birth.

At a very young age, Norbert Rillieux was recognized as an extremely intelligent child. His father, realizing his ability, sent Norbert to Paris, France, to be educated.

As he went through school, Norbert Rillieux excelled in engineering science. As early as 1830, when only 24 years old, he was an instructor in applied mechanics at L'Ecole Centrale in Paris.

By this time, too, Rillieux had published a series of papers on steam engine work and had several inventions to his name. It was also about this time that Rillieux began to develop his idea of the multiple-effect evaporator. He tried, without success, to get several French machinery manufacturers to build a device to try out the idea.

Norbert Rillieux's reputation as a talented engineer somehow reached Louisiana. In New Orleans, a new sugar refinery was being built. The owner of the new refinery approached Rillieux and asked him to become the chief engineer. Disappointed because he could not get French backing for his evaporator, Rillieux decided to try his luck in America. He returned to his homeland in 1830 to accept a job at the sugar refinery.

A Cheaper Sweetener

Rillieux's position as chief engineer of a new sugar factory lasted only a short while. It seems that Vincent Rillieux had a disagreement with the owner of the sugar refinery where his son worked. Norbert resigned from his position to avoid displeasing his father. He did not have a chance to try out his plan, and soon he decided to set out on his own.

Rillieux's first attempt at using a practical evaporator was in a plantation experiment. He had the help of two friends, but the death of one of them prevented him from experimenting any further.

Following this first setback, Rillieux went into the real estate business. He hoped to earn enough money to build and operate his own evaporator. He made an enormous fortune but lost it in a bank failure in 1837. Shortly afterward, however, Rillieux made another attempt at operating a multiple-effect evaporator. This attempt failed, too, for reasons that remain uncertain, but probably because of mechanical difficulties.

Despite these early misfortunes, Rillieux did not quit. Finally, the first of his patents was awarded to him in August 1843.

In the same year, he met Theodore Packwood, a sugar manufacturer who owned a plantation near New Orleans. Packwood was interested in Rillieux's invention. He invited the young inventor to install a multiple-effect evaporator on his sugar plantation.

In 1845, the "Rillieux System" operated with complete success on Packwood's plantation. Most authorities agree that this was the first workable, multiple-effect vacuum evaporator in the world.

Rillieux's apparatus received quick and loud acclaim. The news of his invention was widespread, and it was soon recognized as a great contribution to the sugar industry. Rillieux's evaporating system produced a superior grade of sugar at greatly reduced costs, and several factories in Louisiana began using it.

The primitive method of evaporating sugar juice in a series of open kettles rapidly gave way to Norbert Rillieux's new process—not only in Louisiana, but also in Cuba and Mexico. The progressive factory owners of Louisiana were especially proud of their new methods, and many financial reports noted the use of the new system. It was not long before Norbert Rillieux was the most famous engineer in the state of Louisiana.

The years from 1845 to 1855 were years of triumph for Rillieux. His evaporating equipment was a sharp contrast to that of older methods. In the past, slaves used long ladles to transfer boiling sugar juice from one steaming kettle to another. But with Rillieux's new discovery, one worker operating a few valves moved the hot juice in completely enclosed containers. This saved both labor and steam and prevented the loss of sugar in the process.

Rillieux's system was more than just a switch from hand operation to a mechanical process. It was a complete overthrow of a manufacturing practice that had changed little through the centuries.

In his patent application, Norbert Rillieux described the evaporator as follows:

> A series of vacuum pans, or partial vacuum pans, have been so combined together as to make use of the vapor of the evaporation of the juice in the first to heat the juice in the second, and the vapor from this to heat the juice in the third, which latter is connected with a condenser, the degree of pressure in each successive one being less. . . . The number of syrup pans may be increased or decreased at pleasure so long as the last of the series is in conjunction with the condenser.

Rillieux's evaporator was based on one central idea. Since steam from ordinary water was used for heating sugar juice to evaporate water from it, then the hot vapor (steam) that came from the sugar juice upon evaporation could be used to evaporate a second pan of juice. The evaporation began with ordinary steam from heated water and ended with steam produced from the juice itself.

Below is one of several drawings that accompanied Rillieux's patent. It shows a series of horizontal pans with steam coils. Each pan has the general form and design of a steam locomotive.

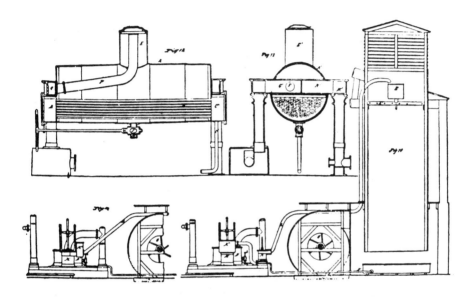

EVAPORATING PAN
Patented 1846

If steam from the first evaporating pan was to be used to heat the juice in the second pan, and so on, then there had to be a difference in temperature between the heating steam (the vapor) and the boiling temperature of liquid to be heated (the juice). Rillieux solved this problem by putting the second and subsequent pans under a vacuum.

A vacuum or partial vacuum is a space that has few air particles in it. The vacuum lowers the air pressure above the juice. This, in turn, lowers its boiling point. When a liquid reaches its boiling point, it evaporates or turns into a gas. In the case of liquid water, the gas is called steam. Water in a pan on your kitchen stove is under normal air pressure and will boil at about 100° C (212° F).

However, suppose you carried your pan of water to the top of a high mountain. At great heights, the air pressure is less because there are fewer air particles in the atmosphere. Since the air pressure is lower, the water would change into steam (evaporate) at a temperature less than 100° C.

Sugar juice boils at 90° C under 23 units of vacuum, at 80° C under 40 units of vacuum, and at 70° C under 52 units of vacuum. The higher the vacuum, the lower the boiling point. The vacuums that Rillieux built into his evaporator created a temperature difference between the heating steam and the boiling point of the juice. So by putting those pans that followed the first pan under partial vacuum, it was possible to use the steam from the first pan to heat the juice in the second, to use the steam from the second to heat the third pan of juice, and so on. This is what is meant by multiple-effect evaporation.

The advantage of such an arrangement can easily be seen. If one pound of coal yields five pounds of steam in the first pan, these five pounds of steam will evaporate another five pounds of steam. These second five pounds will evaporate still another five pounds. In such a way, with four consecutive pans, 20 pounds of water would be evaporated by the burning of only one pound of coal.

The key to Rillieux's invention was his understanding of the nature of steam. He managed the repeated use of latent heat. "Latent" means "not visible or apparent." The steam resulting from the evaporation in the first pan contains practically all of the latent heat of the original steam used to heat the first batch of juice. This is so because liquids absorb heat when they evaporate and become a gas. It was this heat that Rillieux tapped and carried over to the second pan.

The latent heat was then used to heat the juice in the second pan. This juice was then able to boil (evaporate) at a lower temperature due to the reduced pressure above the juice caused by the vacuum. At the end of the third evaporating pan, there was a condenser that cooled the steam, changing it back into water.

Not only did Norbert Rillieux's multiple use of latent heat result in a saving of fuel, but the lower evaporating temperatures reduced the risk of the crystallizing sugar becoming discolored from excessive heat.

Days of Disappointment

Before Norbert Rillieux began work on his evaporator, two other inventors had developed the vacuum pan and condensing coils. The vacuum pan, invented in 1813, was modified by Rillieux. DeGrand, a French inventor, built an evaporator that condensed the steam from the vacuum pan using cool sugar juice. But DeGrand's system did not properly use the latent heat of the vapors. It remained for Norbert Rillieux to modify what had been tried before him, putting some old and new ideas together into a successful combination.

Sometime after 1855, Norbert Rillieux left Louisiana and returned to France. Some believe that he did not want to leave, that he did so only because of the racial prejudice and discrimination faced by African Americans. Rillieux's professional status was solid. He was one of the most prestigious engineers in the state of Louisiana. However, though his ideas, ability, and achievements were accepted, Norbert Rillieux was not treated equally because of his racial ancestry.

When Rillieux was employed on various sugar plantations as a consulting engineer, the "color problem" was met by providing him special living quarters. Because he was black, Rillieux could not be entertained in the plantation owners' homes or in the homes of any other white people. Although there are no records of Rillieux being unjustly treated in America, his secretary in France noted that Rillieux battled against prejudice for 13 years before he could build his first multiple-effect evaporator.

In the United States during the 1850s, free blacks were being more and more restrained. Though they never reached the very low status of slaves, free black people were subjected to restrictions and ridicule. By 1855, they could not even walk the streets of New Orleans without permission. A traveling black person could not stop off in

New Orleans unless represented by a white person. It is quite probable that the social conditions faced by African Americans during the pre-Civil War days made Rillieux decide to return to France.

Not only was Norbert Rillieux's social status lowered because of his color, but at least one of his engineering achievements was probably ignored because of his race. He worked out a practical plan for a sewerage system for the city of New Orleans, but local authorities at the time refused to accept and adopt it. Many people believe that Rillieux's plan was never accepted because of the racial prejudice that existed at the time.

Curiously, it was back in France, where there was little racial discrimination, that Rillieux faced even more trouble with his inventions and patents. It seems that a German who once worked for the firm in Philadelphia that constructed Rillieux's first multiple-effect evaporator had copied the plans. From these designs, the first evaporator in France was installed in a sugar beet factory in 1852.

But due to a complete misunderstanding of Rillieux's designs, this evaporator and others constructed like it in Europe operated very poorly. The engineers who tried to use his designs apparently lacked the scientific knowledge needed to build and operate the evaporator that Rillieux had invented in America.

So when Rillieux reached France in the late 1850s, he had a bad name among the French sugar engineers. He could not find anyone interested in trying his sugar refining process.

Completely discouraged, Norbert Rillieux lost interest in sugar engineering and machinery. He turned instead to archaeology and spent the next 10 years in this profession. In 1880, a leading sugar planter from New Orleans visited Paris and was surprised to find that Rillieux was hard at work translating Egyptian writing in a library.

And then, for some unknown reason, at the age of 75, Rillieux renewed his interest in his evaporator. He sought to obtain a patent for his system of manufacturing sugar from the sugar beet plant. He was finally successful in 1881. The French sugar beet houses had at last accepted Rillieux's efforts, and he received full credit for cutting their fuel costs in half. Yet the experts still refused to acknowledge that the multiple-effect evaporating process was created by Rillieux back in the 1840s—and that it had worked. Again, he retired from the work to which he had contributed so much.

Even at the time of his death in 1894, Rillieux was still active and alert. According to Rillieux's best friend, "He died more from a broken heart than from the weight of years."

Sweet Remembrance

Through time, Norbert Rillieux's place in America's history of industrial science and technology has been lost. If the historical sources mention him at all, they rarely mention the fact that Rillieux was a black man. In fact, in most of the biographical histories of American inventors, Norbert Rillieux is completely ignored.

In 1914, a Dutch sugar expert published a paper on evaporation. He was impressed by Rillieux's work in the field and decided to start a movement to give worldwide recognition to him. He gathered together other authorities in the sugar processing industry, including the president of the International Society of Sugar Cane Technologists. Together, they contacted sugar companies throughout the world for contributions to a memorial in honor of Rillieux.

The response was very enthusiastic in support of the work done by Rillieux. There were 38 contributors to the memorial, representing practically every sugar cane and sugar beet producing company in the world.

If you ever visit the Louisiana State Museum in New Orleans, you will see a plaque from representatives of the sugar industry. The plaque has a relief bust of Norbert Rillieux. Its inscription reads:

> To honor and commemorate
> Norbert Rillieux
> Born at New Orleans, La., March 18, 1806
> and died at Paris, France
> October 8, 1894.
> Inventor of Multiple Evaporation and its
> Application into the Sugar Industry
> This tablet was dedicated in 1934 by
> Corporations representing the
> Sugar Industry all over the world.

GRANVILLE T. WOODS

8

On January 14, 1886, an article in the *Catholic Tribune* (Cincinnati, Ohio) called Granville T. Woods "equal, if not superior, to any inventor in the country." Woods' invention of a railway telegraph system, it was claimed, would "revolutionize the mode of street car transit." The article continued:

> The results of his experiments are no longer a question of doubt. He has excelled in every possible way in all his inventions. He is master of the situation, and his name will be handed down to coming generations as one of the greatest inventors of his time. He has not only elevated himself to the highest position among inventors, but has shown beyond doubt the possibility of a colored man inventing as well as one of any other race.

About a year later, in April 1887, the same paper added to its praise of Granville Woods:

> Mr. Woods, who is the greatest electrician in the world, still continues to add to his long list of electrical inventions. The latest device he invented is the Synchronous Multiplex Railway Telegraph. By means of this system, the railway dispatcher can note the position of any train on the route at a glance. The system also provides means for telegraphing to and from the train while in motion. . . . In using the devices, there is no possibility of collision between trains, as each train can always be informed of the position of the other while in motion.

Earlier, in 1887, the *Cincinnati Colored Citizen*, in its January 29 issue, ran a similar article:

> We take great pleasure in congratulating Mr. G. T. Woods on his success in becoming so prominent that his skill and knowledge of his chosen art compare with that of any one of our best electricians of the day.

At the time these articles appeared, the Woods' Railway Telegraph Company was located in Cincinnati, Ohio. These generous tributes showed how proud Cincinnati's citizens were of one of their own. But they also reflected the real electro-mechanical genius of Granville T. Woods. During his lifetime, he was awarded some 50 patents for his various inventions. Most of these were devices that had to do with the control and distribution of electricity. However, Woods was a versatile man, and some of his patents were in non-electrical fields as well.

More than a dozen inventions by Woods improved the railways. They included an electro-mechanical brake, new methods of tunnel construction for an electric railway, and an electric railway conduit. In 1892, hundreds of children who visited the famous Coney Island amusement park in New York rode on a miniature electric railway that Woods invented. The small train was something very new. It had no exposed wires and required no secondary batteries.

The electric current used to run the train was taken from iron blocks placed at intervals between the rails. By an ingenious arrangement of magnets and switches, the current was turned on only at those blocks passed over by the moving cars.

In addition to his electric railway devices, Granville Woods had many other electrical inventions to his credit. They included improvements in telegraphy, a phonograph, telephone instruments, an automatic cut-off for electric circuits, and a regulator for electric motors.

Perhaps Woods' most noteworthy electrical invention was his induction telegraphy, a system that was designed to send telegraphic messages to and from a moving train. This was important in the 1800s because it could help to prevent collisions by keeping the crew of a train informed of the location of the train that was immediately ahead or following it.

The Making of a Mechanic

How did Granville Woods come to make such a major contribution to electrical technology?

Granville T. Woods was born in Columbus, Ohio, in 1856. He attended school there until he was 10 years old. At this young age, he began working in a machine shop that repaired railroad equipment. It was at that time that his lifelong interest in railroads began.

As a boy, Woods was always anxious to learn. The mysteries of electricity intrigued him, and he read every book he could find on the subject. From each department in the machine shop where he worked, he tried to learn as much as he could about electrical engineering. With part of his weekly earnings, he paid for private instruction from the master mechanic at the shop. His basic mechanical and electrical knowledge was increased by many other jobs he held. What he learned at one job helped him to get and work at another.

In 1872, when he was 16 years old, Granville Woods headed west. After some difficulty in finding a job, Woods obtained one as a fireman, a worker who stokes the fire on a train, on the Iron Mountain Railroad in Missouri. (He went on to become an engineer for the railway line.)

While working for the railroad, Granville Woods had plenty of leisure time, and he spent all of it studying and experimenting with electricity. Shortly afterward, Woods moved to the town of Springfield, Illinois. There, he was employed at a mill where iron and steel were rolled into plates and bars.

When he was 20, Woods left Illinois and headed east to attend a technical school. For two years, he received training in electrical and mechanical engineering. Even while attending school, he worked a six-and-a-half-day week. His days were spent in a machine shop. During the evenings, he attended classes.

In 1878, after completing his two-year course, Woods went to sea as an engineer aboard the *Ironsides*, a British steamer. He was able to visit nearly every continent in the world. After two years, he went back to railroads, this time handling a steam locomotive for a railroad company in Cincinnati, Ohio.

During his years of travel and study, Woods had often been denied work because he was a black man. He never let this situation depress him for long. However, despite his studies and hard work, racial prejudice held him back. Even with his experience and training, he was prevented from advancing in the engineering jobs that he held. So Woods finally decided to open his own shop to work on and sell the inventions he had in mind.

The Key to Communication

Because of his many successful electrical inventions, Woods is often compared to the inventor Thomas Edison. In fact, he is sometimes called the "Black Edison."

In the early stages of his career, he organized the Woods Electric Company in Cincinnati. This business took over many of Woods' early patents, and from 1884 on his inventions began to multiply both in number and value each year.

As his reputation in the electrical-engineering world grew, Woods found that some of the largest corporations in the United States were interested in his work, companies such as General Electric, Westinghouse, American Bell Telephone, and American Engineering.

The Bell Telephone company purchased from Woods a device for transmitting messages by electricity. Here is how Woods described the invention:

> In the ordinary mode of sending telegraphic messages, the operator uses a "finger-key" to irregularly make and break the circuit or to vary the tension of the electric current traversing the "line-wire," the "key" being operated by the varying pressure of the operator's finger. This key as ordinarily constructed cannot be operated in any other way or for any other purpose than just mentioned. The message thus transmitted is received by an instrument known as a "receiver" or "sounder," which causes audible atmospheric vibrations in response to the pulsations of the electric current traversing the line-wire.
>
> It is well known that both the sender and the recipient of messages thus transmitted must be skilled operators. It is also well known that the sounder as usually constructed will not respond to very weak electric currents, such as used in telephony. My system (called by me "Telegraphony") entirely overcomes the failings of the ordinary key and sounder and has a wide range of usefulness, it being capable of use by inexperienced persons—for if, for example, the operator cannot read or write the Morse signals, he has only (by means of a suitable switch) to "cut" the battery out of the main-line circuit and "cut" into a local circuit and then speak near the key. This having been done, the sounder at the receiving station will cause the air to vibrate in unison with the electric pulsations that traverse the line-wire. The person at the receiving-station will thus receive the message as articulate speech.

Another of Granville Woods' inventions was a device for regulating electric motors. In an electric motor, electrical energy is changed into energy of motion or mechanical energy. Many of the machines in your home (such as a vacuum cleaner, a washing machine, or a food mixer) are run by electric motors. With electrical power, it is necessary at times to change the speed of the rotating shaft of a motor without changing or disturbing the electrical voltage at its source.

Until the time of Woods' invention, changing the speed of the shaft was done by adding coils of electrically resistant wire to the motors. These coils, called resistances, would drain off some of the electricity coming into the motor. But they became hot very quickly, like the electric coils in a bread toaster, and using them was really a waste of electricity.

By using a complicated device called a dynamotor, Woods was able to reduce the size of the resistances. This lessened the loss of electricity and greatly reduced the chance of overheating.

Certain parts of his motor regulator were challenged by rival inventors. In 1895, hearings were held at the U.S. Patent Office to establish the true inventor. As it turned out, only one of the rival inventors had his invention even partly completed.

The Patent Office investigation proved that Woods had obviously developed his invention first because there was no other prior model for him to follow or copy. In fact, by the time Woods completed his model, the other inventors were just beginning theirs, and it was much later before they eventually developed similar devices.

Through his business activities and patent defenses, Granville Woods became quite knowledgeable about the legal aspects regarding inventions. Woods' electric motor regulator was not the only invention he had to defend. His most famous invention—the induction telegraph, a system for communicating to and from moving trains—was also contested by a rival inventor who had been working on a similar system.

Getting the Message Across

During the 1800s, newspapers were filled with reports of collisions between railway trains in all sections of the country. Frequently, a train would run into the one ahead of it on the track. Some way of warning an approaching train had to be found. Many methods of signaling between moving trains and stations had been tried. Many engineers believed that a solution could be found in the field of electrical science since electricity could be used to send messages along wires.

Because electricity moves very rapidly along a conducting wire, these impulses are received almost at the same time they are sent. Telegraphy was the first method used to send messages by electricity. "Telegraphy" is a Greek word meaning "to write at a distance"—in other words, to send news by signals to distant places. The first telegraph system was invented by Samuel Morse in 1837.

The simplest telegraph system consists of a battery for a supply of electricity, wires for conducting electricity, a key, and a sounder. The key is a special apparatus for sending messages (electrical impulses); the sounder is a piece of equipment that receives the messages. Messages are sent by tapping out words, letter by letter, with the telegraph key. The letters are then received at the other end as a "click" or "buzz" sound. Using a code (the International Morse Code), the duration of the sounds (long and short) can be translated into letters making up the words of the message.

The use of telegraphy had helped to reduce the number of train accidents. The various types of telegraphic equipment required human operators, one on the train and one at the train station. Telegraph messages between the two operators kept each informed about the location of the trains on the track.

Even so, there were still accidents. During heavy fog, the signalman could hardly see beyond the station. The railway signalmen, being human, were capable of error. At night, a lone signalman at a station could easily become drowsy and fall asleep. Some sort of system was needed that would not rely solely on one telegraph operator at the train station.

The improvement of electric telegraphy made possible what was called the "Block System." The railways were divided into blocks or sections. A train could not leave one block and enter the next until it received an "all clear" message over the telegraph line. This system was used in special sections of the track such as long tunnels.

Although the "Block System" had a good record of preventing accidents, some serious collisions still occurred for sometimes the automatic signals failed to work. When this happened, a station telegraph operator would often become flustered and send out unclear messages over the telegraph. This mix-up would often result in two trains colliding in the same block.

There was a more basic problem with train telegraphic equipment. Any telegraph set-up required a continuous wire connection between the key and the sounder. Thus, some part of the moving trains had to be in direct contact with the conducting wire between the telegraph equipment in the station and that on the train. Only under favorable conditions did the best of these train telegraphic systems work. And many times the messages were incomplete or interrupted because the metal contact between the moving train and the conducting wire was poor.

Granville Woods developed a system of train telegraph signaling that did not depend on contact between some part of the moving train and the conducting wire to the station. He designed a system that used the principle of electrical induction, hence the naming of his invention as the Induction Telegraph System.

Before looking more closely at Woods' invention, let's look at the principle of electrical induction.

Suppose you had a length of wire that was conducting electricity. Let's call it the primary wire. Now, suppose you placed another length of wire like the first, parallel and close to, but not touching, the primary wire. The electric current in the primary wire causes, or induces, electricity to flow into the second wire.

Induction telegraphy was not discovered by Woods, but it was his idea to use it in a railroad telegraph system.

What Woods did was to lay an electric wire between the rails. Each end of this ground wire was connected to a battery and a telegraph key and sounder at the station. In one of the cars on the train, there were also a battery, key, and sounder. Underneath the train car containing this equipment was suspended an electric cable. It ran the length of the car and was connected only to the telegraph equipment inside the car. This cable was 8 to 10 inches above and parallel to the wire that ran along the ground between the rails.

When messages, as impulses of electricity, were sent into the cable suspended from the car, an electric current was induced into that portion of the ground wire directly under the moving car. The strength of the induced current was strong enough so that it could be picked up by the receiving apparatus at the station.

In the same way, electrical impulses generated at a train station and passed into the ground wire were picked up by the cable attached to the train as it moved over the ground wire. No metallic connection or direct contact was needed between the moving train and the station telegraph equipment. A train, either in motion or at rest, could thus receive messages from a station in back of or in front of it. Likewise, a moving or resting train could send messages to a station.

Granville Woods' patent for his telegraph system was not easily won. Another inventor who had been working on a system similar to his challenged Woods' patent. In two Patent Office cases, Woods was declared the inventor.

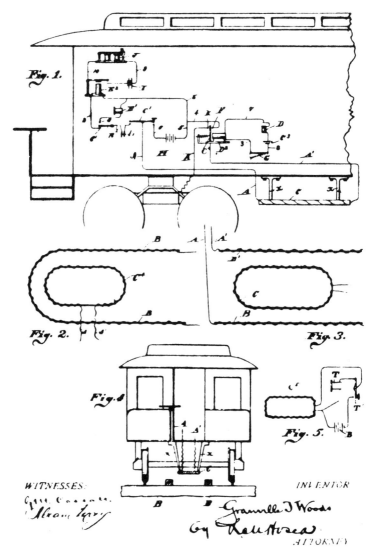

RAILWAY INDUCTION TELEGRAPH SYSTEM
Patented 1887

Granville Woods' new telegraph system helped to eliminate train collisions.

In his patent application, Granville Woods described his Induction Telegraph System:

> My invention relates to systems of electric communication between two moving railway trains or vehicles, or between the same and a fixed station or stations, and transmits the signals to and from the vehicle by means of induction, whereby an electric impulse upon the line-conductor is caused to produce a corresponding impulse upon the similarly arranged conductor carried by the vehicle in close proximity to the line-conductor. . . .
>
> Any code of signals may be employed in my system of communication. A telephone-receiver and a telegraph-relay may be arranged so that either one may cut into the circuit when a signal is to be received.

Creative Genius

In completing and patenting his different inventions, Granville Woods appears to have surpassed every other black inventor of his time in the number and variety of his inventions. This record lasted for over a quarter of a century, until Woods passed away in 1910.

In 1917, an article titled "The Negro in the Field of Invention" appeared in the *Journal of Negro History*. It was written by Henry E. Baker, an assistant examiner at the U.S. Patent Office in Washington, D.C. The article paid a fitting tribute to Granville Woods:

> So far as the writer is aware, there is no inventor of the colored race whose creative genius has covered quite so wide a field as that of Granville T. Woods, nor one whose achievements have attracted more universal attention and favorable comment from technical and scientific journals both in this country and abroad.

VALERIE L. THOMAS
AND OTHER WOMEN INVENTORS

9

When Valerie Thomas was eight years old, the first book she borrowed from the public library was *The Boy's First Book on Electronics*. She was excited about finding this book, and she had high expectations that her father would help her with some of the projects in it. It was her father's tinkering with radios and television sets that had sparked her early interest in electronics.

When she returned the book to the library, Valerie found *The Boy's Second Book on Electronics*, which she also took home with the same expectations. But her father did not offer to help her. The book sat on the shelf in her bedroom until it was due back at the library. Her curiosity about how a radio transmits sound and how a television set produces a picture on the screen was not satisfied.

Nor was her curiosity satisfied at the all-girls high school that Valerie attended in her home city of Baltimore, Maryland. The school didn't offer courses in electronics. Valerie Thomas was disappointed, but not discouraged.

Although she was an excellent mathematics student, Valerie did not take the advanced math courses offered as electives in high school. Not taking advanced math was "the most fatal mistake" of her academic career, Valerie Thomas admits. She had to study hard and work overtime at Morgan State University to make up for those courses so that she could complete her degree in physics. At Morgan State, she was one of only two women in her class majoring in physics.

Despite some discouragement along the way and a subtle message that technology and mathematics "were not for girls," Valerie Thomas became an accomplished data analyst and mathematician. She has excelled in the field of computer technology.

Today, Thomas is the assistant chief of the Space Science Data Operations Office at the National Aeronautics and Space Administration's Goddard Space Flight Center (GSFC) in Greenbelt, Maryland.

The "Real" Thing

In 1980, Valerie Thomas received a U.S. patent as the inventor of the illusion transmitter.

To understand her invention, we must understand something about optics, the study of the mechanics or behavior of light, and illusions. When light rays bounce off a solid object, like a box or a person, our eyes capture the real object as an image, or a likeness, of the real thing. An illusion, on the other hand, only appears to be real. In fact, if you tried to touch the object, it would not be there.

A flat mirror, like the one in your bathroom, produces what is called a virtual image. The image appears to be inside or behind the mirror. The light rays reflected off a concave mirror's surface make the image appear to be real—that is, formed in the space out in front of the mirror. This image can look as real as the object being reflected. You would have to try to touch this image to be convinced that it is only a reflection, or an illusion.

Thomas' invention is a "three-dimensional illusional television system for transmitting an illusion of an object." The invention makes use of the concept of real images. The application of Valerie Thomas' idea may one day be as common as televisions and computers are today.

Imagine your favorite entertainer moving around in your own living room while he or she was performing in a studio miles away. Or imagine shopping for the latest clothing fashions by having them appear before your eyes as you sit at home.

Just an Illusion

How does the illusion transmitter work?

The device is a system for transmitting real images (see the left figure in the illustration) and recreating them on the receiving end (see the right figure in the illustration). It includes a concave mirror on the transmitting end for creating the real images for transmission and a concave mirror on the receiving end for recreating the real image after receiving it. The object—a box—is labeled "14" in the illustration below; the image or illusion of the box is labeled "23" in the illustration. This system would pick up signals the same way your television set does.

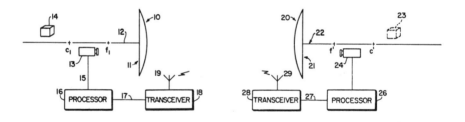

ILLUSION TRANSMITTER
Patented 1980

It took a great deal of effort to figure out how such a transmitter would work. In 1977, while Valerie Thomas was experimenting with the new transmitter, she received the help of an able assistant—her five-year-old son, Mark, who helped Thomas to set up the equipment and observe the relationship between the object and the real image relative to their positions from the concave mirrors.

Since 1964, Thomas has been a mathematician as well as a data analyst for the National Aeronautics and Space Administration (NASA). She has designed computer data systems to support satellite control centers.

Valerie Thomas has also worked on the development of Landsat image processing systems for more than 10 years. Landsat was the first satellite to produce images from outer space that are used to study and preserve our planet's land resources.

Valerie Thomas was the GSFC technical expert in the Landsat Ground Station Operators Working Group, an international group. One of Valerie Thomas' accomplishments was her leadership of the GSFC team that supported the Large Area Crop Inventory Experiment. This experimental program used space technology to help predict crop yields on a worldwide basis. She was also the assistant program manager for Landsat/Nimbus at NASA headquarters.

As project manager for the Space Physics Analysis Network (SPAN) in the late 1980s, Valerie Thomas helped to develop a revolutionary new tool for scientific research. SPAN is a computer network that connects thousands of computers, nationally and internationally.

This network has enabled users in the United States, Canada, South America, and Europe to communicate with each other and access satellite data. SPAN was a major advance in helping scientists who use satellite data to do research on world climates, the sun, astrophysics, oceanography, and earth science.

While Valerie Thomas was the project manager, SPAN supported research related to a supernova explosion, Halley's comet, ozone hole studies, and Voyager satellite encounters with the planets Uranus and Neptune. Hers has been a unique and prolific career.

Simple Curiosity

Valerie Thomas did not set out to make electronics her career goal. It was simple curiosity that motivated her to pursue technical studies. "I've always been curious about what makes things tick," she has said.

It was this curiosity that led to her invention.

In 1976, at a scientific exhibit, Valerie Thomas saw, in her words, "a dramatic and puzzling" demonstration of an illusion. A glowing light bulb had been unscrewed and removed from a socket, and yet it appeared to her eyes that the bulb was still there and lit.

"I could still see the bulb," a surprised Thomas said. "I had to walk up to it and try to touch it to convince myself that it really wasn't there."

Thomas was experiencing an illusion. A second bulb pointing downward in a socket beneath the top socket was still lit and in place. A concave mirror had been used to produce the illusion of the removed bulb. Thomas asked herself what was behind this intriguing demonstration.

Just as she did when she was in elementary school. Thomas marched off to the library to study. She devoured books on optics, as many years earlier she had read "boys" books on electronics. She learned how a concave mirror can be used to create an illusion. Once she figured out what was happening in the light bulb demonstration, she got the idea for her own invention. What fun it would be, Thomas thought, if these illusions could appear in the space of her living room or den at home.

African-American Women Inventors

African-American women like Valerie Thomas have been demonstrating creativity and problem-solving skills for a long time. As you can see from the listing of some of these inventors in Appendix B, they have received patents in a broad range of fields beginning as far back as 1885.

Just as African-American men faced discrimination in getting new ideas tried and accepted because of their race, so these women faced the same obstacle. In addition, they had to confront the prejudice that women who enter scientific fields often encounter.

Until recent years, mechanical and other technical areas were thought to be "for men only." Women were not expected or encouraged to be interested in technology and were generally excluded from studies and opportunities in these areas.

So African-American women have had three hurdles to overcome: getting people to accept their inventions (a hurdle that all inventors must face) and the double dose of prejudice they received due to the fact that they were both black and female.

Ellen Elgin is an example of someone who met the challenge. In the 1880s, Elgin, who lived in Washington, D.C., invented a clotheswringer. A member of the Women's National Industrial League, Elgin sold her invention to an agent for $18.

The wringer was a financial success. When asked why she sold the invention after giving years of her time to its development, Elgin replied:

> You know I am black, and if it was known that a Negro woman patented the invention, white ladies would not buy the wringer. I was afraid to be known because of my color in having it introduced in the market—that is the only reason. I am working on another invention and have money to push it after the patent is issued to me. And the invention will be known as a black woman's, too. I am looking forward to exhibiting the model at the Women's International Inventors Congress, to which women are invited to participate regardless of color.

While the inventions of African-American women have been small in number, they have been quite diverse—from simple domestic devices to complex mechanical items, from beauty aids to health-care products. And while most of these women had no mechanical or technical training, they did have both the creative spirit and the determination that drives the great inventors.

Practical Answers

Five African-American women received U.S. patents between 1885 and 1898. The first was Sarah E. Goode, of Chicago, Illinois, who designed a folding bed similar to today's sofa bed. The second patent awarded to an African-American woman went to Miriam E. Benjamin in 1888 for a "Gong and Signal Chair." The chair was equipped with both a small flag (signal) and a bell (gong). They could be activated by a rod secured to the seat of a chair and within reach of the hand. In a hotel dining room, this system could be used to beckon a waiter for service.

Benjamin's gong-and-signal system was used in the U.S. House of Representatives for signaling pages to come to the seats of congressmen. Before this invention was adopted, the pages were called by members clapping their hands, and the noise disturbed the House proceedings. With Benjamin's device, a congressman quietly pushed a button on his chair. The button rang a small gong and displayed a signal on the back of the chair.

Four years after Benjamin received her patent, Anna Mangin, of Woodside, New York, received a patent for a pastry fork. In her patent claim, Mangin noted that her invention was "for pressing and cutting and pulverizing dry pastry." That same year, a patent was awarded to Sarah Boone, of New Haven, Connecticut, for an ironing board "having its edges curved to correspond to the outside and inside seams of a sleeve."

Keeping the strands of yarn from being tangled while knitting was a problem solved by Julia F. Hammonds. Her "Apparatus for Holding Yarn Skeins," patented in 1896, was described as a device "for use in winding yarns and silks." The entire device was fitted to the chair where the knitter sat.

In 1898, a new hairbrush was patented. It permitted easy cleaning by having a detachable unit for the bristles. Its inventor was Lyda D. Newman, of New York City.

Almost 18 years passed before the work of another African-American woman was recognized with a patent. In 1916, Madeline Turner, of Oakland, California, invented a fruit press. Turner's invention provided a new method for extracting juice from apples, pears, and other fruits.

To keep each room warm in the building she owned, Alice H. Parker created a heating furnace for which she received a patent in 1919. The furnace heated the building at a temperature individually selected for each room. Her invention used gas as fuel and carried hot air to different rooms. It had heating units that branched out from a central mechanism, with each unit being controlled independently. Individual hot-air ducts went to different rooms in the building or house. The system saved energy and money by heating only the space requiring heat.

Beauty culture—hair and skin care—was an interest and a business for many African-American women in the early 1900s. It was natural, therefore, that new hair care products would result as the women in the "beauty business" looked for better methods and materials.

In 1928, Marjorie S. Joyner, of Chicago, received a patent for a "Permanent Waving Machine," a device that could put waves in the hair of both white and black people. At the time, Joyner was employed by the Madame C. J. Walker Manufacturing Company. In the early 1900s, Walker had developed new hair preparations and an ironing comb that was used to straighten the hair of black people. Walker had also developed lotions for skin care. Her beauty products made Madame Walker a millionaire.

In the 1940s, Henrietta Bradberry exhibited inventive talent in two quite different areas. As a housewife, Bradberry claimed that she had time "to work out ideas to perfection." Her "Bed Rack," patented in 1943, was an attachment to a bed that allowed air to circulate around worn clothes to refresh them while a person was sleeping. In a completely different area, inventor Bradberry became interested in military equipment during World War II. She developed a "Torpedo Discharge Means," patented in 1945. This device, by using compressed air, would discharge a torpedo from below the surface of a body of water.

Mary B. D. Kenner was granted the largest number of patents of any African-American woman. Between 1956 and 1987, she was awarded five patents for devices ranging from health aids to bathroom conveniences. Her first two patented inventions (awarded in 1956 and 1959) were for sanitary belts. In 1966, Kenner's third patent was for a "Carrier Attachment for Invalid Walkers." In 1982, she received a patent for a new bathroom tissue holder. Her invention made it easier to grasp the free end of the paper. In 1987, Kenner was given a patent for a "Back Washer." Her device was affixed by suction cups to a shower wall or back of a tub. A user would rub the surface of his or her back over a fabric cover that was soaped and wet.

Kenner started inventing as a high-school student in Washington, D.C. She observes that invention "runs in the family." Her father had several patented inventions. "So I inherited it," Kenner says. "I don't do it for the money. I just can't stop inventing."

Kenner's sister, Mildred A. Smith, is also an inventor. Smith designed a game for teaching family relationships and history. She received a patent for her genealogical game for young people, called the Family Relationships Card Game, in 1980.

In the 1960s, Julia Carter received her patent for a nursery chair. Carter and her husband did a lot of traveling by automobile with their six young children, and the frequent stops to use the rest rooms were, as she put it, "just plain inconvenient." It slowed down the trips.

"I sat up late at night for many nights thinking about my idea and sketching it on paper," recalled Carter. "The first model cost only $75 to have built, . . . but being a black woman, it was difficult to get anyone to invest in its manufacturing." Carter's chair was the size of a portable typewriter and had a storage pan that could hold the waste material until there was a chance to empty the pan.

Three African-American female inventors of the 1970s were Gertrude Downing, Virgie M. Ammons, and Mary A. Moore. Downing's invention (co-patented with William P. Desjardin) was a household item—a "Reciprocating Corner and Baseboard Cleaning Auxiliary Attachment for Rotary Floor Treatment Machines," patented in 1973. The attachment was designed to be used with a rotary floor washer and buffer so that the baseboard and the corners of the room could be cleaned and polished, too.

Another creative device for the home—a "Fireplace Damper Actuating Tool"—was patented by Virgie Ammons in 1975. Her mechanism made it easier to open and close the metal plate that controls the flow of air needed in a home fireplace.

In 1979, Mary Moore was recognized for her development of a pain reliever. This chemical substance (called a "Pain Relief Composition") was made from two different plant root materials to which isopropyl alcohol was added.

When Maxine Snowden, of Washington, D.C., couldn't find a rain hat to keep her hair looking attractive when going to work on rainy days, she invented her own rain hat. She received a U.S. patent for her design in 1983. The Patent Office record describes her rain hat as follows: "The covering area puffs to loosely enclose the wearer's hair while the front and rear peripheries fit snugly against the wearer's head generally adjacent the hairline."

Far too often, the achievements of African-American women inventors have been overlooked. African-American women have successfully contributed to a field commonly thought of as "a man's business."

Their work should remind us that there is no need for "inventor" to be considered a masculine word.

APPENDIX A:
SOME NOTABLE AFRICAN-AMERICAN
INVENTORS BEFORE 1900

Inventor	Invention	Date
Abrams, W.B.	Hame Attachment	Apr. 14, 1891
Allen, C.W.	Self-Leveling Table	Nov. 1, 1898
Allen, J.B.	Clothesline Support	Dec. 10, 1895
Ashbourne, A.P.	Process for Preparing Coconut for Domestic Use	June 1, 1875
Ashbourne, A.P.	Biscuit Cutter	Nov. 30, 1875
Ashbourne, A.P.	Process of Treating Coconut	Aug. 21, 1877
Bailes, W.	Ladder Scaffold Support	Aug. 5, 1879
Bailey, L.C.	Combined Truss and Bandage	Sept. 25, 1883
Bailey, L.C.	Folding Bed	July 18, 1899
Bailiff, C.O.	Shampoo Headrest	Oct. 11, 1898
Ballow, W.J.	Combined Hat Rack and Table	Mar. 29, 1898
Barnes, G.A.E.	Design for Sign	Aug. 19, 1898
Beard, A.J.	Rotary Engine	July 5, 1892
Beard, A.J.	Car Coupler	Nov. 23, 1897
Becket, G.E.	Letter Box	Oct. 4, 1892
Bell, L.	Locomotive Smokestack	May 23, 1871
Bell, L.	Dough Kneader	Dec. 10, 1872
Benjamin, L.W.	Broom Moistener and Bridle	May 16, 1893
Benjamin, M.E.	Gong and Signal Chair for Hotels	July 17, 1888
Binga, M.W.	Street-sprinkling Apparatus	July 22, 1879
Blackburn, A.B.	Railway Signal	Jan. 10, 1888
Blackburn, A.B.	Spring Seat for Chairs	Apr. 3, 1888
Blackburn, A.B.	Cash Carrier	Oct. 23, 1888

Blair, H.	Corn Planter	Oct. 14, 1834
Blair, H.	Cotton Planter	Aug. 31, 1836
Blue, L.	Hand Corn-shelling Device	May 20, 1884
Booker, L.F.	Design Rubber Scraping Knife	Mar. 28, 1899
Boone, S.	Ironing Board	Apr. 26, 1892
Bowman, H.A.	Making Flags	Feb. 23, 1892
Brooks, C.B.	Punch	Oct. 31, 1893
Brooks, C.B.	Street Sweeper	Mar. 17, 1896
Brooks, C.B.	Street Sweeper	May 12, 1896
Brooks, H. & P.	Street Sweeper	Apr. 21, 1896
Brown, H.	Receptacle for Storing and Preserving Papers	Nov. 2, 1886
Brown, L.F.	Bridle Bit	Oct. 25, 1892
Brown, O.F.	Horseshoe	Aug. 23, 1892
Brown & Latimer	Water Closet for Railway Cars	Feb. 10, 1874
Burkins, E.	Rapid-Fire Gun	
Burr, J.A.	Lawn Mower	May 9, 1899
Burr, W.F.	Switching Device for Railways	Oct. 31, 1899
Burwell, W.	Boot or Shoe	Nov. 28, 1899
Butler, R.A.	Train Alarm	June 15, 1897
Butts, J.W.	Luggage Carrier	Oct. 10, 1899
Byrd, T.J.	Improvement in Holder for Reins for Horses	Feb. 6, 1872
Byrd, T.J.	Apparatus for Detaching Horses from Carriages	Mar. 19, 1872
Byrd, T.J.	Improvement in Neck Yokes for Wagons	Apr. 30, 1872
Campbell, W.S.	Self-Setting Animal Trap	Aug. 30, 1881
Cargill, B.F.	Invalid Cot	July 25, 1899

Carrington, T.A.	Range	July 25, 1876
Carter, W.C.	Umbrella Stand	Aug. 4, 1885
Certain, J.M.	Parcel Carrier for Bicycles	Dec. 16, 1899
Cherry, M.A.	Velocipede	May 8, 1888
Cherry, M.A.	Streetcar Fender	Jan. 1, 1895
Church, T.S.	Carpet-beating Machine	July 29, 1884
Clare, O.B.	Trestle	Oct. 9, 1888
Coates, R.	Overboot for Horses	Apr. 19, 1892
Cook, G.	Automatic Fishing Device	May 30, 1899
Coolidge, J.S.	Harness Attachment	Nov. 13, 1888
Cooper, A.R.	Shoemaker's Jack	Aug. 22, 1899
Cooper, J.	Shutter and Fastening	May 1, 1883
Cooper, J.	Elevator Device	Apr. 2, 1895
Cooper, J.	Elevator Device	Sept. 21, 1897
Cornwell, P.W.	Draft Regulator	Oct. 2, 1888
Cornwell, P.W.	Draft Regulator	Feb. 7, 1893
Cosgrove, W.F.	Automatic Stop Plug for Gas Oil Pipes	Mar. 17, 1885
Cralle, A.L.	Ice-cream Mold	Feb. 2, 1897
Creamer, H.	Steam Feed Water Trap	Mar. 17, 1885
Creamer, H.	Steam Trap	Mar. 8, 1887
Creamer, H.	Steam Trap	Jan. 17, 1888
Creamer, H.	Steam Trap Feeder	Dec. 11, 1888
Creamer, H.	Steam Trap	May 28, 1889
Creamer, H.	Steam Trap	Aug. 18, 1891
Creamer, H.	Steam Trap	Nov. 21, 1893
Darkins, J.T.	Ventilation	Feb. 19, 1895
Davis, I.D.	Tonic	Nov. 2, 1886
Davis, W.D.	Riding Saddle	Oct. 6, 1896
Davis, W.R., Jr.	Library Table	Sept. 24, 1878

Deitz, W.A.	Shoe	Apr. 30, 1867
Dickinson, J.H.	Pianola	
Dorsey, O.	Door-holding Device	Dec. 10, 1878
Dorticus, C.J.	Device for Applying Colorful Liquids to Sides of Soles or Heels of Shoes	Mar. 19, 1895
Dorticus, C.J.	Machine for Embossing Photo	Apr. 16, 1895
Dorticus, C.J.	Photographic Print Wash	Apr. 23, 1895
Dorticus, C.J.	Hose Leak Stop	July 18, 1899
Downing, P.B.	Electric Switch for Railroad	June 17, 1890
Downing, P.B.	Letter Box	Oct. 27, 1891
Downing, P.B.	Street Letter Box	Oct. 27, 1891
Dunnington, J.H.	Horse Detacher	Mar. 16, 1897
Edmonds, T.H.	Separating Screen	July 20, 1897
Elkins, T.	Dining, Ironing Table and Quilting Frame Combined	Feb. 22, 1870
Elkins, T.	Chamber Commode	Jan. 9, 1872
Elkins, T.	Refrigerating Apparatus	Nov. 4, 1879
Evans, J.H.	Convertible Settee	Oct. 5, 1897
Faulkner, H.	Ventilated Shoe	Apr. 29, 1890
Ferrell, F.J.	Steam Trap	Feb. 11, 1890
Ferrell, F.J.	Apparatus for Melting Snow	May 27, 1890
Ferrell, F.J.	Valve	May 27, 1890
Ferrell, F.J.	Valve	Apr. 14, 1891
Ferrell, F.J.	Valve	Nov. 10, 1891
Ferrell, F.J.	Valve	Jan. 26, 1892
Ferrell, F.J.	Valve	Feb. 2, 1892
Ferrell, F.J.	Valve	Feb. 9, 1892
Ferrell, F.J.	Valve	Jan. 17, 1893
Ferrell, F.J.	Valve	July 18, 1893

Fisher, D.A.	Joiners' Clamp	Apr. 20, 1875
Fisher, D.A.	Furniture Caster	Mar. 14, 1876
Flemming, R.F., Jr.	Guitar	Mar. 14, 1876
Goode, S.E.	Folding Cabinet Bed	July 14, 1885
Grant, G.F.	Golf Tee	Dec. 12, 1899
Grant, W.S.	Curtain Rod Support	Aug. 4, 1896
Gray, R.H.	Bailing Press	Aug. 28, 1894
Gray, R.H.	Cistern Cleaner	Apr. 9, 1895
Gregory, J.	Motor	Apr. 26, 1887
Grenon, H.	Razor Stropping Device	Feb. 18, 1896
Griffin, F.W.	Pool Table Attachment	June 13, 1899
Gunn, S.W.	Boot or Shoe	Jan. 16, 1899
Haines, J.H.	Portable Basin	Sept. 28, 1897
Hammonds, J.F.	Apparatus for Holding Yarn Skeins	Dec. 15, 1896
Harding, F.H.	Extension Banquet Table	Nov. 22, 1898
Hawkins, J.	Gridiron	Mar. 26, 1845
Hawkins, R.	Harness Attachment	Oct. 4, 1887
Headen, M.	Foot Power Hammer	Oct. 5, 1886
Hearness, R.	Sealing Attachment for Bottles	Feb. 15, 1898
Hilyer, A.F.	Water Evaporator Attachment for Hot Air Registers	Aug. 26, 1890
Hilyer, A.F.	Register	Oct. 14, 1890
Holmes, E.H.	Gage	Nov. 12, 1895
Hunter, J.H.	Portable Weighing Scale	Nov. 3, 1896
Hyde, R.N.	Composition for Cleaning and Preserving Carpets	Nov. 6, 1888
Jackson, B.F.	Heating Apparatus	Mar. 1, 1898
Jackson, B.F.	Matrix Drying Apparatus	May 10, 1898
Jackson, B.F.	Gas Burner	Apr. 4, 1899

Jackson, H.A.	Kitchen Table	Oct. 6, 1896
Jackson, W.H.	Railway Switch	Mar. 9, 1897
Jackson, W.H.	Railway Switch	Mar. 16, 1897
Jackson, W.H.	Automatic Locking Switch	Aug. 23, 1898
Johnson, D.	Rotary Dining Table	Jan. 15, 1888
Johnson, D.	Lawn Mower Attachment	Sept. 10, 1899
Johnson, D.	Grass Receiver for Lawn Mowers	June 10, 1890
Johnson, I.R.	Bicycle Frame	Oct. 10, 1899
Johnson, P.	Swinging Chair	Nov. 15, 1881
Johnson, P.	Eye Protector	Nov. 2, 1880
Johnson, W.	Egg Beater	Feb. 5, 1884
Johnson, W.	Velocipede	June 20, 1899
Johnson, W.A.	Paint Vehicle	Dec. 4, 1888
Johnson, W.H.	Overcoming Dead Center	Feb. 4, 1896
Johnson, W.H.	Overcoming Dead Center	Oct. 11, 1898
Jones & Long	Cap for Bottles	Sept. 13, 1898
Joyce, J.A.	Ore Bucket	Apr. 26, 1898
Latimer, L.H.	Manufacturing Carbon	June 17, 1882
Latimer, L.H.	Apparatus for Cooling and Disinfecting	Jan. 12, 1886
Latimer, L.H.	Locking Rack for Hats, Coats, and Umbrellas	Mar. 24, 1896
Lavalette, W.A.	Printing Press	Sept. 17, 1878
Lee, H.	Animal Trap	Feb. 12, 1867
Lee, J.	Kneading Machine	Aug. 7, 1894
Lee, J.	Bread Crumbing Machine	June 4, 1895
Leslie, F.W.	Envelope Seal	Sept. 21, 1897
Lewis, A.L.	Window Cleaner	Sept. 27, 1892
Lewis, E.R.	Spring Gun	May 3, 1887

Linden, H.	Piano Truck	Sept. 8, 1891
Little, E.	Bridle Bit	Mar. 7, 1882
Loudin, F.J.	Sash Fastener	Dec. 12, 1892
Loudin, F.J.	Key Fastener	Jan. 9, 1894
Love, J.L.	Plasterers' Hawk	July 9, 1895
Love, J.L.	Pencil Sharpener	Nov. 23, 1897
Marshall, T.J.	Fire Extinguisher	May 26, 1872
Marshall, W.	Grain Binder	May 11, 1886
Martin, W.A.	Lock	July 23, 1889
Martin, W.S.	Lock	Dec. 30, 1890
Matzeliger, J.E.	Mechanism for Distributing Tacks	Nov. 26, 1899
Matzeliger, J.E.	Nailing Machine	Feb. 25, 1896
Matzeliger, J.E.	Tack Separating Mechanism	Mar. 25, 1890
Matzeliger, J.E.	Lasting Machine	Sept. 22, 1891
McCoy, E.	Lubricator for Steam Engines	July 2, 1872
McCoy, E.	Lubricator for Steam Engines	Aug. 6, 1872
McCoy, E.	Lubricator	May 27, 1873
McCoy, E.	Steam Lubricator	Jan. 20, 1874
McCoy, E.	Ironing Table	May 12, 1874
McCoy, E.	Steam Cylinder Lubricator	Feb. 1, 1876
McCoy, E.	Steam Cylinder Lubricator	July 4, 1876
McCoy, E.	Lubricator	Mar. 28, 1882
McCoy, E.	Lubricator	July 18, 1882
McCoy, E.	Lubricator	Jan. 9, 1883
McCoy, E.	Lawn Sprinkler Design	Sept. 26, 1899
McCoy, E.	Steam Dome	June 16, 1885
McCoy, E.	Lubricator	June 16, 1885
McCoy, E.	Lubricator	Feb. 8, 1887
McCoy, E.	Lubricator Attachment	Apr. 19, 1887

McCoy, E.	Lubricator for Safety Valves	May 24, 1887
McCoy, E.	Lubricator	May 29, 1888
McCoy, E.	Dope Cup	Sept. 29, 1891
McCoy, E.	Lubricator	Dec. 29, 1891
McCoy, E.	Lubricator	Mar. 1, 1892
McCoy, E.	Lubricator	Apr. 5, 1892
McCoy, E.	Lubricator	June 6, 1893
McCoy, E.	Lubricator	Sept. 13, 1898
McCoy, E.	Lubricator	Oct. 4, 1898
McCoy, E.	Lubricator	Nov. 15, 1898
McCoy, E.	Lubricator	June 27, 1899
McCoy & Hodges	Lubricator	Dec. 24, 1889
McCree, D.	Portable Fire Escape	Nov. 11, 1890
Mendenhall, A.	Holder for Driving Reins	Nov. 28, 1899
Miles, A.	Elevator	Oct. 11, 1887
Mitchell, C.L.	Phoneterisin	Jan. 1, 1884
Mitchell, J.M.	Checkrow Corn Planter	Jan. 16, 1900
Moody, W.U.	Game Board Design	May 11, 1897
Morehead, K.	Reel Carrier	Oct. 6, 1896
Murray, G.W.	Combined Furrow Opener and Stalk Knocker	Apr. 10, 1894
Murray, G.W.	Cultivator and Marker	Apr. 10, 1894
Murray, G.W.	Planter	June 5, 1894
Murray, G.W.	Cotton Chopper	June 5, 1894
Murray, G.W.	Planter	June 5, 1894
Murray, G.W.	Combined Cotton Seed	June 5, 1894
Murray, G.W.	Planter and Fertilizer Distributor Reaper	June 5, 1894
Murray, W.	Attachment	Jan. 27, 1891
Nance, L.	Game Apparatus	Dec. 1, 1891

Nash, H.H.	Life-preserving Stool	Oct. 5, 1875
Newman, L.D.	Hairbrush	Nov. 5, 1898
Newson, S.	Oil Heater or Cooker	May 22, 1894
Nichols & Latimer	Electric Lamp	Sept. 13, 1881
Nickerson, W.J.	Mandolin and Guitar Attachment for Pianos	June 27, 1899
O'Conner & Turner	Alarm for Boilers	Aug. 25, 1896
O'Conner & Turner	Steam Gage	Aug. 25, 1896
O'Conner & Turner	Alarm for Coasts Containing Vessels	Feb. 8, 1898
Outlaw, J.W.	Horseshoe	Nov. 15, 1898
Perryman, F.P.	Caterers' Tray Table	Feb. 2, 1892
Peterson, H.	Attachment for Lawn Mowers	Apr. 30, 1889
Phelps, W.H.	Apparatus for Washing Vehicles	Mar. 23, 1897
Pickering, J.F.	Air Ship	Feb. 20, 1900
Pickett, H.	Scaffold	June 30, 1874
Pinn, T.B.	File Holder	Aug. 17, 1889
Polk, A.J.	Bicycle Support	Apr. 14, 1896
Pugsley, A.	Blind Stop	July 29, 1890
Purdy, W.	Device for Sharpening Edged Tools	Oct. 27, 1896
Purdy, W.	Device for Sharpening Edged Tools	Aug. 16, 1898
Purdy, W.	Device for Sharpening Edged Tools	Aug. 1, 1899
Purdy & Peters	Design for Spoons	Apr. 23, 1895
Purdy & Sadgwar	Folding Chair	June 11, 1889
Purvis, W.B.	Bag Fastener	Apr. 25, 1882
Purvis, W.B.	Hand Stamp	Feb. 27, 1883
Purvis, W.B.	Paper Bag Machine	Feb. 12, 1884

Purvis, W.B.	Fountain Pen	Jan. 7, 1890
Purvis, W.B.	Paper Bag Machine	Jan. 28, 1890
Purvis, W.B.	Paper Bag Machine	June 24, 1890
Purvis, W.B.	Paper Bag Machine	Aug. 19, 1890
Purvis, W.B.	Paper Bag Machine	Sept. 2, 1890
Purvis, W.B.	Paper Bag Machine	Sept. 22, 1891
Purvis, W.B.	Electric Railway	May 1, 1894
Purvis, W.B.	Paper Bag Machine	May 8, 1894
Purvis, W.B.	Paper Bag Machine	Dec. 11, 1894
Purvis, W.B.	Magnetic Car Balancing Device	May 21, 1895
Purvis, W.B.	Paper Bag Machine	Mar. 9, 1897
Purvis, W.B.	Electric Railway Switch	Aug. 17, 1897
Queen, W.	Guard for Companionways and Hatches	Aug. 18, 1891
Ray, E.P.	Chair Supporting Device	Feb. 21, 1899
Ray, L.P.	Dustpan	Aug. 3, 1897
Reed, J.W.	Dough Kneader and Roller	Sept. 23, 1884
Reynolds, R.R.	Nonrefillable Bottle	May 22, 1899
Reynolds, H.H.	Window Ventilator for Railroad Cars	Apr. 3, 1883
Reynolds, H.H.	Safety Gate for Bridges	Oct. 7, 1890
Rhodes, J.B.	Water Closet	Dec. 19, 1899
Richardson, A.C.	Hame Fastener	Mar. 14, 1882
Richardson, A.C.	Churn	Feb. 17, 1891
Richardson, A.C.	Casket Lowering Device	Nov. 13, 1894
Richardson, A.C.	Insect Destroyer	Feb. 28, 1899
Richardson, A.C.	Bottle	Dec. 12, 1899
Richardson, W.H.	Cotton Chopper	June 1, 1886
Richardson, W.H.	Child's Carriage	June 18, 1899

Richey, C.V.	Car Coupling	June 15, 1897
Richey, C.V.	Railroad Switch	Aug. 3, 1897
Richey, C.V.	Railroad Switch	Oct. 26, 1897
Richey, C.V.	Fire Escape Bracket	Dec. 28, 1897
Richey, C.V.	Combined Hammock and Stretcher	Dec. 13, 1898
Rickman, A.L.	Overshoe	Feb. 8, 1898
Ricks, J.	Horseshoe	Mar. 30, 1886
Ricks, J.	Overshoe for Horses	June 6, 1899
Robinson, E.R.	Electric Railway Trolley	Sept. 19, 1893
Robinson, E.R.	Casting Composite	Nov. 23, 1897
Robinson, J.	Dinner Pail	Feb. 1, 1887
Robinson, J.H.	Life-saving Guard for Locomotives	Mar. 14, 1899
Robinson, J.H.	Life-saving Guard for Streetcars	Apr. 25, 1899
Romain, A.	Passenger Register	Apr. 23, 1889
Ross, A.L.	Runner for Stops	Aug. 4, 1896
Ross, A.L.	Bag Closure	June 7, 1898
Ross, A.L.	Trousers Support	Nov. 28, 1899
Ross, J.	Bailing Press	Sept. 5, 1899
Roster, D.N.	Feather Curler	Mar. 10, 1896
Ruffin, S.	Vessel for Liquids and Manner of Sealing	Nov. 20, 1899
Russell, L.A.	Guard Attachment for Beds	Aug. 13, 1895
Sampson, G.T.	Sled Propeller	Feb. 17, 1885
Sampson, G.T.	Clothes Dryer	June 7, 1892
Scottron, S.R.	Adjustable Window Cornice	Feb. 17, 1880
Scottron, S.R.	Cornice	Jan. 16, 1883
Scottron, S.R.	Pole Tip	Sept. 21, 1886
Scottron, S.R.	Curtain Rod	Aug. 30, 1892

Scottron, S.R.	Supporting Bracket	Sept. 21, 1893
Shanks, S.C.	Sleeping Car Berth Register	July 21, 1897
Shorter, D.W.	Feed Rack	May 17, 1887
Shrewcraft, F.	Letter Box	
Smith, J.W.	Improvement in Games	Apr. 17, 1900
Smith, J.W.	Lawn Sprinkler	May 4, 1897
Smith, J.W.	Lawn Sprinkler	Mar. 22, 1898
Smith, P.D.	Potato Digger	Jan. 21, 1891
Smith, P.D.	Grain Binder	Feb. 23, 1892
Snow & Johns	Liniment	Oct. 7, 1890
Spears, H.	Portable Shield for Infantry	Dec. 27, 1870
Standard, J.	Oil Stove	Oct. 29, 1889
Standard, J.	Refrigerator	July 14, 1891
Stewart, E.W.	Punching Machine	May 3, 1887
Stewart, E.W.	Machine for Forming Vehicle Seat Bars	Mar. 22, 1887
Stewart, T.W.	Mop	June 13, 1893
Stewart, T.W.	Station Indicator	June 20, 1893
Stewart & Johnson	Metal Bending Machine	Dec. 27, 1887
Sutton, E.H.	Cotton Cultivator	Apr. 7, 1874
Sweeting, J.A.	Device for Rolling Cigarettes	Nov. 30, 1897
Sweeting, J.A.	Combined Knife and Scoop	June 7, 1898
Taylor, B.H.	Rotary Engine	Apr. 23, 1878
Taylor, B.H.	Slide Valve	July 6, 1897
Thomas, S.E.	Waste Trap	Oct. 16, 1883
Thomas, S.E.	Waste Trap for Basins, Closets, etc.	Oct. 4, 1887
Thomas, S.E.	Casting	July 31, 1888
Thomas, S.E.	Pipe Connection	Oct. 9, 1888
Toliver, G.	Propeller for Vessels	Apr. 28, 1891

Tregoning & Latimer	Globe Supporter for Electric Lamps	Mar. 21, 1882
Walker, P.	Machine for Cleaning Seed Cotton	Feb. 16, 1897
Walker, P.	Bait Holder	Mar. 8, 1898
Waller, J.N.	Shoemaker's Cabinet or Bench	Feb. 3, 1880
Washington, W.	Corn Husking Machine	Aug. 14, 1883
Watkins, I.	Scrubbing Frame	Oct. 7, 1890
Watts, J.R.	Bracket for Miner's Lamp	Mar. 7, 1893
West, E.H.	Weather Shield	Sept. 5, 1899
West, J.W.	Wagon	Oct. 18, 1870
White, D.L.	Extension Steps for Cars	Jan. 12, 1897
White, J.T.	Lemon Squeezer	Dec. 8, 1896
Williams, C.	Canopy Frame	Feb. 2, 1892
Williams, J.P.	Pillow Sham Holder	Oct. 10, 1899
Williams, P.B.	Electromagnetic Electrical Railway Track Switch	Apr. 24, 1900
Winn, F.	Direct Acting Steam Engine	Dec. 4, 1888
Winters, J.R.	Fire Escape Ladder	May 7, 1878
Winters, J.R.	Fire Escape Ladder	Apr. 8, 1879
Woods, G.T.	Steam Boiler Furnace	June 3, 1884
Woods, G.T.	Telephone Transmitter	Dec. 2, 1884
Woods, G.T.	Apparatus for Transmission of Message by Electricity	Apr. 7, 1885
Woods, G.T.	Relay Instrument	June 7, 1887
Woods, G.T.	Polarized Relay	July 5, 1887
Woods, G.T.	Electro-Mechanical Brake	Aug. 16, 1887
Woods, G.T.	Telephone System and Apparatus	Oct. 11, 1887
Woods, G.T.	Electromagnetic Brake Apparatus	Oct. 18, 1887

Woods, G.T.	Railway Telegraphy	Nov. 15, 1887
Woods, G.T.	Induction Telegraph System	Nov. 29, 1887
Woods, G.T.	Overhead Conducting System for Electric Railway	May 29, 1888
Woods, G.T.	Electromotive Railway System	June 26, 1888
Woods, G.T.	Tunnel Construction for Electric Railway	July 17, 1888
Woods, G.T.	Galvanic Battery	Aug. 14, 1888
Woods, G.T.	Railway Telegraphy	Aug. 28, 1888
Woods, G.T.	Automatic Safety Cutout for Electric Circuits	Jan. 1, 1889
Woods, G.T.	Electric Railway System	Nov. 10, 1891
Woods, G.T.	Automatic Safety Cutout for Electric Circuits	Oct. 14, 1889
Woods, G.T.	Electric Railway Supply System	Oct. 31, 1893
Woods, G.T.	Electric Railway Conduit	Nov. 21, 1893
Woods, G.T.	System of Electrical Distribution	Oct. 13, 1896
Woods, G.T.	Amusement Apparatus	Dec. 19, 1899
Wormley, J.	Life-saving Apparatus	May 24, 1881

APPENDIX B:
SOME NOTABLE AFRICAN-AMERICAN
WOMEN INVENTORS

Inventor	*Invention*	*Date*
Ammons, V.M.	Fireplace Damper Actuating Tool	Sept. 30, 1975
Benjamin, M.E.	Gong and Signal Chair for Hotels	July 17, 1888
Boone, S.	Ironing Board	Apr. 26, 1892
Bradberry, H.	Bed Rack	May 25, 1943
Bradberry, H.	Torpedo Discharge Means	Dec. 11, 1945
Brown, M.V.B.	Home Security System	Dec. 2, 1969
Carter, I.O.	Nursery Chair	Feb. 9, 1960
Cowans & Hall	Embroidered Fruit Bowl Wall Hanging and Kit	Apr. 5, 1977
Downing, G.	Reciprocating Corner Baseboard Cleaning Auxiliary Attachment for Rotary Floor Treatment Machine	Feb. 13, 1973
Goode, S.E.	Folding Cabinet Bed	July 14, 1885
Griffin, B.V.	Portable Receptacle Support	Mar. 24, 1951
Hammonds, J.F.	Apparatus for Holding Yarn Skeins	Dec. 15, 1896
Holmes, L.M.	Knockdown Wheeled Toy	Nov. 14, 1950
Joyner, M.	Permanent Waving Machine	Nov. 27, 1928
Kenner, M.B.D.	Sanitary Belt	May 15, 1956
Kenner, M.B.D.	Sanitary Belt with Moistureproof Napkin Pocket	Apr. 14, 1959
Kenner, M.B.D.	Carrier Attachment for Invalid Walker	May 18, 1976
Kenner, M.B.D.	Bathroom Tissue Holder	Oct. 19, 1982
Kenner, M.B.D.	Back Washer Mounted on Shower Wall and Bathtub	July 29, 1987

Mangin, A.M.	Pastry Fork	Mar. 1, 1892
Moore, M.A.	Pain Relief Composition and Method of Preparing Same	Dec. 4, 1979
Newman, L.D.	Hairbrush	Nov. 5, 1898
Parker, A.H.	Heating Furnace	Dec. 23, 1919
Smith, M.E.	Family Relationships Card Game	Oct. 28, 1980
Snowden, M.	Rain Hat	Mar. 5, 1983
Thomas, V.L.	Illusion Transmitter	Oct. 21, 1980
Toland, M.	Float-Operated Circuit Closer	May 4, 1920
Turner, M.M.	Fruit Press	Apr. 25, 1916

INDEX

ABOUT THE AUTHOR

An educator, historian, and author, Robert C. Hayden is known nationally for his writing, lecturing, and teaching on the history of African Americans. He is the author of *Black in America: Episodes in U.S. History* (1969) and *African Americans in Boston: More than 350 Years* (1991). He was a contributor to *Dictionary of American Negro Biography* (1982). From 1974 to 1983, his weekly column, "Boston's Black History," appeared in the *Bay State Banner* in Boston. In 1986, he wrote a viewer's guide to the television series "Eyes on the Prize: America's Civil Rights Years, 1954 to 1965."

Hayden's first biography for young readers, *Singing for All People: Roland Hayes*, was published in 1989. His other books include *Faith, Culture and Leadership: A History of the Black Church in Boston; Boston's NAACP History: 1910 to 1982;* and *The African Meeting House in Boston: A Celebration of History.*

A member of the Executive Committee of the Association for the Study of Afro-American Life and History and president of the Boston branch of the association, Hayden is also a lecturer in the Department of African-American Studies at Northeastern University and in the Black Studies Program at Boston College. In addition, he holds adjunct faculty positions at Bentley College and Curry College.

Hayden is president of RCH Associates, an educational consulting firm that works with school and community groups to develop awareness of African-American life and history and to foster intergroup understanding and communication.

Hayden served as executive director of the Massachusetts Pre-Engineering Program from 1987 to 1991.

From 1980 to 1982, Hayden was employed by the Boston Public Schools, where he held several administrative positions: special assistant to the superintendent, executive assistant to the superintendent, and director of project development. He also served as director of the Secondary Technical Education Project at the Massachusetts Institute of Technology.

From 1970 to 1973, he served as executive director of the Metropolitan Council for Educational Opportunity in Boston and then worked in educational research and development at the Educational Development Center in Newton, Massachusetts.

During the early years of his career, Hayden was a science teacher, a news writer for *Current Science*, and a science editor in the educational division of Xerox Corporation.

Hayden earned his B.A. in 1959 and a master's degree in 1961, both from Boston University. He has also completed two post-graduate fellowships: one in the School of Education at Harvard University (1965-1966), the other in the Department of Urban Studies and Planning at the Massachusetts Institute of Technology (1976-1977).

Robert Hayden is the author of three volumes in "Achievers: African Americans in Science and Technology." This biography series includes *11 African-American Doctors*, *9 African-American Inventors*, and *7 African-American Scientists*. First published in the 1970s, these books have now been revised, expanded, and updated by the author.